A Nice Cup of tea and a Biscuit

- The Memoirs of Beverly Merrin Dempsey as told to

P.B. Holmes.

*I would like to dedicate this book to my Mum, Pauline Barbara Froggatt.
I will never be able to thank her for the wonderful support she gave me through life.
I miss her more and more each day
Also to my two sons Joseph Damon Cochrane and Jason Cochrane and my Father   Edward Peter Froggatt.*

Contents.

Chapter 1 Small Ads
Chapter 2 Where it all began
Chapter 3 The Teenage Years
Chapter 4 Lashing Out
Chapter 5 On Remand
Chapter 6 Bang Clang Bang Clang
Chapter 7 Crown Court
Chapter 8 Maternity Ward
Chapter 9 The Blushing Bride
Chapter 10 Beauty Queen
Chapter 11 New Men in my Life
Chapter 12 Back in Prison
Chapter 13 Escaping to France
Chapter 14 Stepping up a Gear
Chapter 15 Going it Alone
Chapter 16 Surprises
Chapter 17 Men
Chapter 18 A Star is Born
Chapter 19 Switch on Bev TV
Chapter 20 My biggest support, My Rock, My Mum
Chapter 21 Reflections.

A Nice cup of tea and biscuit.

The memoirs of Beverly Merrin Dempsey.

Chapter 1 - Small Ads.

I sat on my bed in my tiny flat, looking at my old black and white photographs. They were the precious memories of my life, they laid there on the bed, looking back at me. If I was the photo image of me looking back at the woman I had become, I think I would have been shocked. When you are little, growing up in the Essex country side, you imagine life is going to turn out so much different to how it has. A single woman in her 40s, in a tiny flat with no money, a poorly paid job, just able to cover the bills with nobody there for me.

The smell of damp engulfed your senses. It did not matter how may windows I left opened, the stench would follow you around the flat. Wallpaper was peeling off the walls and the boiler would only supply hot water for the shower intermittently. It was all I could afford, it was an address but that was all. Once again, another relationship had finished and once again I was the on rocks. No money, nowhere to go and snapping up the first affordable place I found.

My choice of men in my life had always gone wrong, I was too trusting and then depended on them too much. Once that support walked out I was always left with nothing. Next to my photographs were the last few coppers from my purse. So, few I didn't even bother to count them. I could not face another plain pasta meal, so cheap yet filling, to sustain through another night of tears and wondering where it all went wrong.

I had to move back to Essex from France after, yet another relationship had imploded and here I am again looking to start my life anew again. Why does this happen to me? I am in my 40s, I have two grown up sons, I should be settled, enjoying life and making the most of my family. But no, here I am in a flat, with no cooker, earning £3.00 per hour in various jobs, struggling to pay the rent, the bills and all other life costs that are thrown at me. Something had to change. My son sat with me as I searched the classifieds for a better job, a path to a better way of life. He had moved in with me from Newcastle, after his relationship had broken down. We were both a sorry state for sore eyes and finding it difficult to dig our way out of this hole.

I knew I was getting desperate when colleagues at the betting shop I worked at dared me to bare my boobs at work for a Daily Star campaign. The sort of thing you would imagine being done in that rag, but I did it. I rang them up and said, "How much I would love to get my tits out at work." I can't even remember why I agreed to do it. Maybe it would be nice positive attention or lead to something else. I was clearly unhappy with life and this just seemed to break the daily monotony of serving old gits in the shop who smelt of booze and cigarettes. Also, I was dared, that's always a big thing for me, I always take on a dare, just to prove I am not scared of anything. It all made sense at the time as the photographer came down to the betting shop in Southend. We set up outside the counter and when I was ready I lifted my top revealing my breasts. Screams of delight from the other shop workers and no sooner had I flashed them, they were once again safely covered under my top.

I actually got quite a buzz from it, I like the positive attention I did get. The photographer was soon gone and here I was again starting another soul-destroying shift taking betting money. Don't get me wrong, I have always been a hard grafter but when you work three jobs and still have barely any money to live, you have to take stock of your life. Something had to change.

I sat on my bed with the local newspaper, I read every single job vacancy available. Most of them I either couldn't do, not experienced or was not qualified to apply for. My heart sunk. I rustled the paper more, turning page after page until I came to the small ads.

> *"Escorts Wanted. Good rates of pay please telephone for more information"*.

I read it again, and wondered if it was me? Escorts, going to dinner with gentlemen, escorting them to events, maybe even on a holiday. I like the company of men, despite all my bad decisions in the past I am sure I could do that. I had managed to salvage nice clothes when leaving my last partner, I know I scrub up well, I can be very sexy and a good talker, I get on with anyone usually.

I rang the number, Ricky answered the phone. I asked about the Escorts agency and after a few questions about my age, looks and how much time I can give he agreed to take me on. I did feel good, but also was still unsure if this was the right thing for me to do. He said he would collect me at 10am the next morning and I was to wear a suit.

I didn't sleep at all that night. I agreed for a strange man to come to my door, drive off with him and then meet other strange men. I panicked, I thought I should ring him, say it was all a mistake. It really was not for me. Then the thought of earning my whole week's wages in a few hours hit me. Just do it this once and then I will have a few quid behind me to pay for a good shop load and rent and then that will buy me more time to get a better paid job. Yes, that's all I will do, I settled down and cat napped and before I knew it morning was here.

I got up, I couldn't eat, just coffee, then another coffee until I felt more human. I showered, put on my makeup and brushed my hair all nicely so I was presentable and waited.

I was collected soon after, I felt good in my suit all made up and looking forward to having a day out in the car, having lunch and dinner with various clients, I was anxious yet excited. Ricky was not quite as I imagined from our telephone conversation. He was short, Indian but treated me with a lot of respect.

"OK Bev, I am taking you to Mr Smith's house, and from there we will do the rounds."

"The rounds?"

"Yes, the rounds." He replied

"Well what's the rounds then?"

"Well Mr Smith, he wants his thing for one hour, Mr. Jones wants full sex 1 hour also....." And so, the list went on.

I was shocked, but knew there was no backing out now, I needed that money. It was so strange hearing a list of names and what they wanted me to do to them or me. So cold and matter of fact. I had always enjoyed sex, but this seemed to be soulless almost robotic in nature. I had to accept it, even if it's just for today, I needed this to help me back on my feet financially.

"We best stop off at the chemist then, hadn't we?" I calmly replied, but shaking in my high heels.

"Yes, lots to be getting on with today so we best get going," he replied.

We set off in the along the Essex roads, till we got to Mr. Smith's place. It was a flat above a pub. I sat in the car, clutching my hand bag to my lap, wondering how the hell my legs were going to get me up those stairs. Amazingly as if on auto pilot, I got out of the car and made my way to the pub. I started looking around to see if anyone was watching. How could they be? There is only three of us that know about this and what if someone knew? It's none of their bloody business.

I got to the front door and knocked. A rather normal looking guy opened and showed me the way in, he could see I was nervous and he tried to calm me by offering me a cup of tea which I accepted, and we chatted. He actually seemed like a really nice guy and I felt I could go through with it with him.

He told me what he wanted, and we made our way to his bedroom. He was already in his dressing gown and soon he was naked. He reached into his dressing table and pulled out a long white club. It was a white sock filled with other white socks. Filled so tight it looked like a massive fabric dildo.

"I am sorry, that's not going in me, "I said. He shook his head and reassured me.

"Oh no, it's for me," and with that he leaped on his bead on all fours and showing me exactly where he wanted it. There I was fully dressed pushing a stuffed sock up a man's arse while he begged me to stop because of the pain. I kept pushing harder and harder and he even pushed back. His face was almost purple with the pain or pleasure he was feeling. He kept screaming as I pulled the sock out and then back in quicker and quicker. My arm just couldn't keep up I wasn't sure which was going to give first his arse or my arm. Thankfully it was his arse. I pulled the shit stained sock out of his arse and he collapsed to his belly. He was totally out of breath the screaming had really tired him out. I felt like I had played 2 hours of tennis and my wrist and elbow were aching like mad. I tried to work out why he would like that? I would hate that being done to my bum, but I guess each to their own.

It was barely 30 minutes in to the hour, but he seemed to have enough. I left with a fistful of cash and got back in the car and off we went to the next appointment. I thought I had seen everything in my life but that was certainly a new experience for me. The image of that sock stayed with me a long time after.

"OK?" He asked. I nodded. "Great let's get going to the next one.

As I finished well within the allotted time for that appointment, we took a slow leisurely drive to the next appointment. Though we drove through some nice countryside, and the weather was lovely I really didn't notice. All I could think about was that huge white cotton dildo grinding in and out of his arse. I was hurting him, I was not even touching him. We didn't kiss, I wasn't even naked all he wanted was this awful pain in his bum. I can still hear his screams and begging today, it really left its mark on me. I really did not understand what I was doing. I was so close to asking Ricky to take me home, but the money I earnt for 30 mins was silly. I will see how the next one goes and then decide what to do.

We pulled up to a large drive of a mock Tudor house. Loads of fake wooden beams and leaded windows. Ricky parked the car behind the front garden hedge, spent a few moments looking at the house and then I saw a head look through the net curtains.

"Okay, Bev, one-hour, full sex and be nice he is a good regular."

"Yeah okay Ricky, I am sure there will be no problems." I got out the car and in my heels walked across the gravelled drive way. I wobbled all the way to the front step, trying my best to look sexy and seductive, a lot easier said than done. I was about to ring the doorbell when the door flew open and the face I saw at the window snarled, "You're early, she has only just left." He ushered me in and told me how his wife had just left the house and we may have seen her on the pavement. I apologised and said I am sorry, and reassured him that no one saw us, and everything would be okay. Soon he was naked, and I was in my underwear and heels with his hands all over my body. Then he was laying on top of me holding onto my shoulders for dear life as he pounded himself inside me. It was nice, – but not nice. I love sex, but I was used to connecting on some level, or at least having some sort of attraction. He kept grabbing me and looking at himself in his wife's dressing table mirror. His grip tightened on my shoulders and soon he fell on me, all sweaty and out of breath. I looked at my watch behind his head as not to look as if I was in a rush to leave and soon realised I had only been there for twenty minutes! I was beginning to wonder if any of them would last the hour?

He got up, the condom waving about between his legs on his limp willy and reached for his dressing gown. In the pocket all nicely rolled up, was the money. He placed it in my hand, saying, "Thanks, be on time next time." I nodded, put my suit on and let myself out. The whole experience left me cold, it wasn't about me, it was about him. I soon realised how mechanical the professional sex act could be. I was just a vessel to use at his will. I had never experienced sex like it, not even bad sex felt this way. It was totally different, and I was not sure it was something I could or should get used to. At least it was not any weird stuff. So that was something to be happy about, in a strange way. More importantly it meant more money in my hand.

So, that's pretty much how my first day went. A different man every hour, some lasted the hour, some couldn't get started at all. It didn't take long before the day became a blur and I just went through the motions, performing for each one to the best of my ability, not wanting to disappoint. My prize was waiting for me at the end of the day, and I did not want anything to happen to stop me from getting it. I needed it, I really needed that money. That is all that kept me going, remembering that small pile of coppers on the bed, not enough to pay for my essentials, I could not face that feeling again. Each man that rolled off and on me was another few notes to that pile. That's all they were, a means to an end.

The day ended at 22:30, over 12 hours of doing the rounds. I was physically exhausted and mentally I felt fragile. I threw the money on the bed, stripped off and got in a bath. I wanted to wash the day off myself. I wanted all the faces I saw on top of me to go away, all the moaning and groaning and the touching and grabbing of me to dissolve into nonexistence. But existed it did, and it was never going to leave me.

My son sat beside me on the toilet and placed his arm around me, as he did so I cried.

Chapter 2 – Where it all began.

My story began in Essex, I was born a healthy happy baby to devoted patents with both sets of grandparents doting on me. My parents were hardworking shop keepers, with four stores in the area selling prams and other baby related items to the local area. Babies must have been popping out here there and everywhere as Mum and Dad were always working hard. Their long hours meant that sometimes I would be looked after by my little grandparents and my big grandparents on alternate weekends so Mum and Dad could keep the business running smoothly.

I called them my little Nan and Granddad and my big Nan & Granddad because that was how they were. Also, my Big Nan and Granddad had my aunt, Cheryl, who was only 3 years older than I, so we spent a lot of time together playing and fighting like children do.

My school years soon crept upon me and I went to a private school in Romford. The school was run by what I can only describe as a French Madam, she was horrible and very strict. The classes were very small, with only 8 or 9 pupils in each. I was one of the smallest in the class but despite this I didn't get let off from the wrath of the French Mistress. She demanded we all play the piano, and if my little fingers did not hit the right notes, my knuckles would be smacked with a ruler until I got it right. I hated her. If you dare to speak in the class, she would walk up behind you at hit you using a big thick text book in the middle of your back. She was evil, a complete bitch and made our lives hell. Luckily, she wasn't the only teacher we had, but when she took our French classes a sense of dread dropped upon the classroom. She was a tyrant.

The school fees for this school were £6 per year, yes that's what my Mum & Dad paid for my education. It was a shame because I hated school. Not only did I hate the tyrant Head Mistress, but I did not do well in the classes themselves. I would get bored and want to be doing other things. I just never seemed to be able to focus on the tasks at hand and over my time there I did not excel in the classroom. I was more a doer than a thinker, I could do loads of practical tasks one after the other if it was over a short period of time. I had a very short attention span which did not help me through those early school years.

When I was 11 I started playing truant. The thought of going to school really did my head in. The days seemed so long, and I really had no interest in what was being taught, or more importantly by the way it was being taught. Just staring at dusty old chalk boards, the teachers going on and on in the same old tone just did not engage me at all. Despite the truancy I never ever got in trouble. If you were at school for registration no one seemed to mind that you were not there the rest of the school day. I would go around to friend's houses and kill the time there. It was much more fun and interesting and as long as I was home in time for dinner, no one seemed to mind.

My education lasted until I was 15 years old. Any exams I took would make my brain freeze and I just did not do well at all. I did like metal work though, I don't know why, I guess it was different and more practical and suited me a lot more than other subjects. One good thing about school was I made lots of good friends, both girls and boys and through my education I formed some excellent stable friendships. In the evenings outside of school, we would go to the youth club. We would go there and for a few hours just dance, listen to music and have a laugh. It was not very structured, we would pay a few pence each visit and hang out with friends.

I would spend a lot of time at my Grandparents house or in Mum & Dads shop. It was there in the hustle and bustle of the business they could keep an eye on me. The shop was a pram shop and a toy store, selling some items for just pennies or a shilling and over time I was allowed to take the money from customers and place the money in the drawer under the counter. There was no till then, just a little wooden drawer under the counter where I could drop in the pennies. I soon learnt about money, adding up and taking away, working out change. I learnt more in the shop then I did at school. I was physically doing something rather than looking in a book, so I found it easier to learn.

As a child all I wanted to do was work with the family in the shops they owned. My Dads Dad had four shops, one in Harold Hill, one in Brentwood, one in Romford and one in Hornchurch where we lived.

Opposite the shop in Hornchurch was a children's home called Cottage Homes. The Shoreditch Guardians of the Poor opened Hornchurch Cottage Homes in 1889. They continued in use as children's homes until 1984, a full 95 years of residential childcare. From what I remember there were thirteen homes there, each one having around 30 children in them. All the children there were orphaned but lived in all these different cottages with various adults. On the site was a swimming pool, tennis courts and lots of other facilities. I would go over there and play with the other kids for a few hours and made friends from there also. As I got older it made realise how lucky I was to have my mum and dad in my life. The main building at the front was a huge game keeper's house, which in the front had a drawer for people to leave babies in when they could no longer look after them. Sometimes the baby would come with a note say, "Please look after me, as my Mummy & Daddy can no longer look after me and my name is...." Knowing how wanted and loved I was at home, I could not even imagine what these poor mothers and fathers would have to go through to place a baby in a drawer like that. It must have been hell for them.

    I had two friends from Cottage homes, one boy called Stephen Pratt and another girl called Sheila. She was a black girl and in those days, that was very unusual, but all seemed quite normal to me as our friendship grew over time. We would hang around on the streets of Hornchurch and she and Stephen would come to our flat above the shop, 172 Hornchurch High St and always be welcomed. We would go to my room and listen to my little red and white record player, listen to 45s and 78s. We would sing and dance and just generally have a lot of fun.

    Another important person in my life was Cheryl. She was my aunt and lived with my Nan & Granddad, she was only 3 years older than me, so we spent a lot of time together growing up. Our relationship was very stormy sometimes and I remember one time when I was caught trying to wash her black cat in the bath (to make it white!). This is resulted in a big fight with Cheryl and I pushed her into the bath, severely hurting her back.

Our relationship never got any better and it worsened as we got older. She was the brainy one and played violin and I wasn't. We were really chalk and cheese. Due to having to spend so much time together we just rubbed each other up the wrong way so fights would ensue.

But despite that, my childhood was a very happy one thanks to my loving family that I had around me.

Chapter 3 - The Teenage Years

When I turned fifteen years old, my Dad decided he wanted to buy a business. It was a garage, called The Red Lion Garage in Stanford le Hope on Red Lion Hill. The business was for selling second hand cars and petrol. Also to one side of the forecourt was a mechanic, so all in all it was a busy place to work. I would serve customers petrol at three shillings and two pence per gallon and look after the money drawer. We would go to car auctions to buy in stock, frequently looking for good deals for the forecourt. I was very close to my Dad, it was great for me to see him trying something new, working hard and getting some sort of decent reward for it all.

Unbeknown to me, during this time my Dad had met up with some people and had started doing some illegal things. I had no idea about this at the time, but my mum suspected that not all my Dads business was legit, so she decided it would be a good time to get herself a place of her own.

Despite the hard work it needed, my Mum had always wanted to run a kennel business. She knew of a kennel whose lease was for sale and she knew this was the right thing to do for myself and her. She had to find £2000 for the yearly payment of the lease and borrowed the money from my grandparents. We moved in and started to try to lick the place in to shape. The whole house was run down and needed so much work to bring it up to a reasonable standard to live in. The main living house had an old open fire in the middle of the room, no kitchen to speak of and very little in the way of creature comforts. Despite this we managed to grow the business. Over time we built up a good regular income, with long term security dogs that we took in, and each day would have to deliver to the Magnets store in Grays. As well as long term boarders, we had short term boarding for dogs who were left behind while their owners travelled to sunnier climes. I got stuck in with the mucking out, walking and feeding of all the dogs and really enjoyed the hard work. One part of the job that used to really upset me was the number of animals that used to get left tied to our gate as they were unwanted. Sometimes even boxes of kittens would be left for us to find and to take in. It ate into our profits but how can you turn these poor little cats and dogs away in their hour of need? In between the daily grind of the dog mucking out I also worked at my Dads garage at the same time. I was busy working hard and loving every moment of it.

After a year my Mum had to find the money to renew the lease again and decided to go to the banks. The Banks were very tough on lending money to women in those days, and one bank after another denied her the loan she needed to continue the business. Despite proving the income could quite easily cover the repayments no one seemed to want to know. Until one day, she tried Barclays Bank, and they agreed that she could easily pay back the money and decided she could have the loan.

This was the best thing that could have ever happened to her. Finally, she had some security of her own, an income and a place to live. While my Dad's business also thrived, and all seemed to be going along rather nicely. I was now 17 years old and life seemed great. I had my friends, my own car, a place to live a job I loved and the loving embrace of my family. My close friend Isabel and I would go out in the car, just to drive around and chat, and go to Romford as I had a few friends in Hornchurch too. It was a hectic life, with very little time to myself so these times spent with friends was a welcome relief from the daily chores.

This perfect bubble I was floating around in was soon going to burst. It had been another day of hard work like any other. Nothing unusual, the dogs were fed and watered and all safely locked away for the night. I was aware of a commotion outside the home and saw my Dad talking to police officers, this was all a great shock to me, I had no idea what this could be about. Soon after he was whisked away in a police car and he did not come home that night.

Unbeknown to us he had taken an opportunity to make easy money by faking bankers' drafts and withdrawing money from the banks. He seemed to have fallen in with the wrong crowd when he took on the garage, and my mother did not seem surprised at all that was happening.

For me all I could see was my world falling apart. I could not believe that my dad could be a criminal, I mean he was my dad, he owned a garage, we were a normal hard-working family. How on earth could this happen? As it turned out, it was pure greed. He had a chance to make quick easy money, and if it sounds too good to be true, then it is too good to be true and my dad fell for it. The next time he went to the police station they held him custody for his court date and he was soon inside prison on remand awaiting his sentence. I was devastated.

He ended up getting five years, he was soon sent to an open prison in Gloucester and I was totally uncertain about anything in my life. I thought dad was the rock of the family, how could he do this? How could he do this to me? I soon began having bad thoughts about life. My life had been turned upside down and nothing seemed to make much sense. Thankfully we had the kennels and the income from that kept us going but my life seemed like it had totally changed.

I visited Dad in prison several times, but things could never be the same. I suddenly produced this rebellious streak, getting into my own wrong crowd that I had met down the local pubs. I wanted to lash out at everyone, I hated authority and from within this small body a huge hatred for the rest of the world grew. My dad had been taken away from me, I didn't care why, I just wanted him back, I wanted everything to be as before. I felt in complete turmoil, my life would never be the same again.

Chapter 4 - Lashing Out.

I was sitting at a badly varnished table in a smoke-filled pub in Rush Green. My Boyfriend, Tony, placed the drinks on it and sat beside me. He was talking to me, but the words just evaporated away in the air like all the cigarette smoke. All I could see was my father's face, solemn with a look of resignation that this was always on the cards. He rode his luck for so long and then the law had to catch up with him. In my eyes he could never do any wrong, the policemen were the wrong doers here, he hadn't hurt anyone, it was just some bad cheques and money from a faceless organisation. The insurance would pay up and it would be like nothing had ever happened. I loved my Dad and this unconditional love clouded my vision of him.

As they bent him over to sit in the Police car with handcuffs behind his back our eyes met for a split second. I wanted to run over and drag him out, they were taking my Dad away, how could they do this? He wasn't an animal, he was a good man, he just wanted to give his family more than he could in his normal day job. The car drove off, I stood there crying with my Mum and felt as if my heart had been pulled from my chest. Over the next few days I realised why my Mum wanted her own independent business. She never wanted to rely on him for anything. It was unusual for a woman to have her own business in those days, but she saw a different side to him than I did and just wanted to protect us from what she always knew would happen. I guess being married to a rogue had its compensations, but she was experienced to know it could not go on forever. For a lady to go to a bank and get a mortgage to buy a business was unheard of. She bought a dog kennels in Essex, it was run down and hard work, but it gave her independence.

After some time and hearing why they arrested him I was still angry. His crimes were still just words they had no meaning what so ever. I wanted my dad back and I wanted us as a whole family again. My whole life was in pieces.

The pub was full of loud people getting drunk, I seemed to be the only one sitting there not laughing and joking. I hated them, there they all were getting intoxicated in the pub while my Dad rots away in prison. I wanted to shout at them all, tell them to shut up but I didn't, I got up nearly knocking the table over and stormed out of the pub. The fresh air did not clear my mind, I knew what I had to do.

I got into my car and sped off down the Essex back lanes, I didn't even care that my boyfriend stayed in the pub chatting to some of his other friends. There were few cars on the road, just the odd set of head lights blinded me now and then. I pulled up to my Mums house and quietly let myself in, Mum was in bed, she was always up early with the dogs in the morning. Above the fire place was a shelf, I grabbed a chair and stood on it and reached for the big lump of cold metal that laid there.

Years before my Dad showed me the shotgun, he always would say to me, "Remember, any problems this is where you find it." He showed me how to release the barrel, so I could slide the cartridges in. The cardboard box of cartridges lay in a drawer in the kitchen. I pulled the gun down, nearly falling off the chair under the weight of it. As I nearly toppled over I used the barrel as a sort of walking stick, if it was loaded I would have blown a huge hole through the floor boards.

Within a minute I was speeding back to the pub in my Mini Van. My new passenger was a shotgun and a box of 22 cartridges, the missing two from the box were sitting in the barrel of the gun. The pub was still heaving when I barged back into the bar area. I pointed as my boyfriend, You, out, now."

Like a lost puppy he followed me outside, as did his two friends, Jimmy Mac and John.

"What's wrong Bev?" he asked, I was breathing heavy, "has something happened?" With an almost growl I replied, "We are going to get our own backs on those bastards who screwed my Dad over."

Tony looked at me and asked, "Who screwed your Dad over?"

I stormed back to car, pulling my arm out of Tony's grip and realised I was not going to get any help from them. In my mind I wanted to hurt the banks and garages that seemed to have lead my dad into temptation. His greed got the better of him and he took the bait. I was definitely not thinking straight, but I had to release my anger on someone or I was going to explode.

I sat in the car, and tried to start it up before the passenger door opened. Tony got inside and then realised he had a huge shotgun in the foot well that almost touched the roof lining.

"Bloody hell Bev, what are you going to do with that?" he shrieked.

"Shut up, I have a score to settle and either you are going to help me or go back in the pub with your chicken mates." The engine started.

"But what we going to do?" He replied.

"I am going to empty those garages of their money, I will show them not mess with us. So, get out if you can't handle it."

"Fucking hell Bev, are you crazy?" I didn't even respond, I just turned the key in the ignition and started the Mini Van up. He started had a big cheesy grin on his face and told me to wait. I thought he wanted me to let him out, but he didn't. He signaled to the others to jump in the back of the van and we sped off into the Essex night.

The three of them seemed to be running on adrenaline, at first, they kept saying that I was mad, and I needed to calm down. When they realised how determined I was to show these bastard garages what they had done to my world the tone changed.

"Let's go back to mine, my Dad's got a gun." We drove to one of the boy's houses and he collected a hand gun, I have no idea what type. It was wrapped up in a cloth and he assured me that the gun was loaded. Then we jumped back in the car and started to look for our first target.

The first garage, was closed. It was late at night - nothing opened at night in those days except pubs. I parked across the street and the four of us got out the van and walked towards the forecourt.

"Bev, its closed we won't get nothing here, let's go."

"Shut up," I replied, "Kick the door down and get us inside." It was then that other two realised I had a huge shot gun.

"What the fuck you going to do with that?" one of them said as Tony aimed the sole of his shoe on the rickety door and with one kick the door flew open. As we walked in I said, "It was to make sure no one tried to stop us." In the fifties and sixties, it was well known that garages were easy targets. I had also worked in one for my Dad for a while, so I knew where the money would be, and the fact that most garages closed after banks did, so they would always have at least a day's takings somewhere on the premises. Also with no CCTV and rickety doors with poor locks, it really was as easy as taking sweets from a baby.

In the garage there were tools, overalls and lots of dust. I knew money would be kept in a drawer at the back of the shop and sure enough there were a few shillings and pence in their little compartments ready for tomorrows trade. I found a locked tin in a cupboard that one of the boys forced opened and I was sure there would be some notes in there. I had to be honest I did not care what we stole, I just wanted them to know that we had been there.

We grabbed anything we felt could be valuable and ran back over to the van. The disappointment in my voice must have showed, I was not content with that, I wanted to hit these bastards hard, I knew it would not happen tonight. I took them back to the pub and made sure they would be ready for tomorrow.

"Oh, come on Bev, this is stupid." Said Jimmy Mac. He was always a little bit edgy and nervous. He suffered with epilepsy and I think he was worried that all this stress running through his body, running around with a crazy girl with a shot gun would set him off. Miraculously it didn't, he reluctantly stuck with us to save face.

"Then don't come then, I bet it won't stop you taking your share of the cash, will it?" I made it clear I would be back to pick them earlier the next day and made sure what I would think of them if they did not turn up. I sped off leaving them behind and went back home. The adrenaline did not die down even when I was in bed, I couldn't sleep. I had nightmares about what I would have done if the was someone behind the counter, would I use the gun? I felt I would have then I had uncertainty shooting through my body, my stomach churned. All I could think about was my dad. He was still gone; my anger was still there.

I still needed revenge.

The next day the four of us were driving around Essex looking for another target. It was glorious sunshine, this time I was definitely going to send a message. Despite my petrol tank being full, we pulled up to the petrol pumps on another remote petrol station. Usually someone would come out to pump the petrol, but no one did.

We stepped out of the car, I was holding the shot gun and Tony the pistol. I heard movement in the shop part of the garage. Tony looked at me and I nodded, this was it. This would be for real. Jimmy Mac opened the door and Tony and John ran in. I followed behind, pointing the shotgun ahead of me. My finger planted firmly on the cold trigger. A middle-aged man stood behind the till, his eyes as wide as they could be with complete fear. It is exactly how I wanted it to be. This man stood their petrified, paying for what had happened to my father.

"Money on the counter NOW." The man did not move, his hands were above his head, his arms shook as if he had a huge weight above him.

"Don't shoot, please, don't shoot."

"MONEY, NOW. ON THE FUCKING COUNTER." I shouted. This poor soul was paying for all my Dad's mistakes, it was not his fault, but my red mist just saw him as part of the problem. Let's see how he likes his life being turned upside down. His hands shook as he tried to get all the notes and change out of the wooden drawer.

"Where's the rest of the float?" I shouted. "Now, get it now." He reached slowly behind him and pulled a tin box with a small lock on it. It rattled with coins, John Snatched it out of his hands and Tony grabbed the money from the counter. The boys started to look for other items to steal, but I felt we had done enough damage here.

"Lay down, Lay down on the floor." The man knelt on his knees and flopped his chest on to the floor. While he was doing that the boys were already on the forecourt, I stood over him with the shot gun pointing at him. I felt every emotion possible in those few seconds, my whole body shook and almost shut down as it did not know what to do. I was standing on a garage with a huge bloody loaded 12 bore shotgun aimed at a man scared out of his wits.

"Stay there." I backed out the shop and then walked slowly towards the Mini. I got in, started it up and drove away nice and slowly. We parked on a layby several miles from the garage. The boys split up the cash, but I sat there gripping the steering wheel. I had no idea how much we stole. I did not care. I stared down the road and still felt anger inside me. It just would not let up. I had to do more. I started the car, much to the shock of the boys and of we headed into the night looking for another garage. Within half hour I found another one. I pulled over across the road from it and parked up.

I watched to see if there was any movement and I could not see a thing. The mechanics side was all locked up and the side shop looked the same. Again, we all got out the van, I pulled the shotgun from the passenger side foot well and we headed to the entrance. Tony put his ear up against the door, he looked and me and shook his head.

"Kick it in, "I shouted, and with a thrust of his boot the door fly opened. As it did so there was a scream from behind the counter.

"Shit," shouted Jimmy Mac. The young woman was in the process of taking off her work jacket and putting on her own coat.

I pointed the gun at her, "Don't make a sound, do you hear?" She stood there frozen, the cold trigger became warm as my hands became sweaty, my arm shook under the weight of the barrel. I pulled in into my shoulder, but I couldn't keep it there, it was too big. Tony then shouted at her to empty the till drawer and give us anything that valuable. She grabbed a bag and poured coins and a note into it. I dropped the gun and held it to my hip, still pointing both barrels at the young lady. She was clearly petrified but I didn't care. The boys ran out the shop and I remained there pointing the gun at her, I was just proving a point, I wanted her to suffer, I wanted to her to suffer like me. I also noticed a huge safe in the far corner of the shop. I kept my gun on her while eyeing up the safe. Of course, all I was doing was frightening the poor girl to death. I backed out the door without saying a word. My arms were shaking, my hands were tight as I tried to put the key in the ignition.

"Come on Bev, let's get out of here." Shouted John. The key clicked round, and the engine jumped into life and soon we were heading down the country lanes back home.

"I want it." I said.

"Want what?" one of the boys replied.

"The safe, we are going back for the safe."

There was uproar in the back of the van, all the reasons why we couldn't go there were shouted at me. It's too soon, the police would be there, but I didn't care. I was on a road to destruction and I didn't care who I was going to take down with me. The boys seemed to do everything I say without question, I expected this from Tony as we were seeing each other but the other two, well they followed me blindly too.

We met up later that night. It was pitch black and the boys were silent. Nothing was said as we drove down the same lanes again. I knew they thought I was mad, going back to the scene of the crime to commit another crime. All I knew was there must be something substantial in that safe and I wanted it.

I stopped the van about one hundred yards down the road from the garage. It was pitch black, not a soul in sight. Not even the Police would think we would return, it was empty. I drove up to the garage again and parked near the entrance for the shop. The door had been secured by some wood, but easy to kick through again. I nodded and with several barges of a shoulder and foot we were inside. There in the far corner was the safe. We stood in front of it, the boys wondering how the hell we were going to open it.

"We won't be able to open it here, get it in the van we will take it home." The shrieks of disbelief echoed around the garage.

"Shut up and get it on the van." They did as they were told and soon all four of us were pushing and pulling the safe across the floor. The tiled floor was being scratched to bits by the safe base. The noise was like finger nails being dragged down a chalkboard. I backed the van up to the door and after several attempts of lifting it from each corner we finally slid into the van.

We all got back in and I started the engine, in our haste we left the door open of the garage and slowly pulled away. The engine struggled with all the weight and soon the noise of the exhaust pipe scraping along the ground got louder and louder. There must have been sparks flying out the back, I slowed down, not that the brakes were all that good. I was now driving in first gear about 5 miles per hour with the loudest scraping noise you could imagine. I just kept thinking about what's in the safe, I just kept the sound out of my head and aimed the car home. Soon the noise stopped, I didn't even notice, but one of the boys in the back saw the exhaust laying in the road behind us, so that was the end of that.

We got to Tony's house and parked in the garage. From the back of the van we finally pushed the safe onto the floor. Barely any of the paint chipped away as it hit the concrete floor. Well into the night we used every one of the tools in the garage to try and open the damn thing. It was sealed tight with a great big handle and keyhole on the door. The noise was deafening, how no one heard us thumping the crap out of this safe I will never know. Everything either bounced off it or snapped while trying to lever the door open. We all stood there bent over double, out of breath. I could hear the boys cursing me, saying I have lost the plot. They were probably right.

There was nothing else for it, we had to lose the safe, it was the biggest piece of evidence in the world, and there it was laying on the garage floor with our prints and hundreds of dents on it. I decided we had to dump it, somewhere safe. The lake.

There was a fishing lake we could back right up to and push it into the water from the van. It was dawn, a beautiful purple and orange glow lit up the Essex sky. Still heavy breathing from getting the safe back onto the van, we pulled up to the lake. I turned the van around, so the back doors were over the water. Then we pushed and pushed till finally the safe sploshed into the water. We sat there quietly to regain our composure, and then I heard, "Oh Shit. Look!"

I turned around and looked out the van through the doors and saw them. A bank of fishermen, all sitting there staring at us. I climbed into the driver's seat and put my head on the steering wheel.

"Shit."

Chapter 5 – On Remand.

I lay in bed awaiting the inevitable. I heard a car pull up near my mum's house and then footstep approaching the front door. I was still in my clothes from the previous night, my Minivan was parked outside, I made no attempt to hide had done the night before. Everything was swirling around in my head. Even though I had done something incredibly stupid, I felt numb to it. I really didn't care, my boyfriend followed me with his friends like idiots and they also will also pay for these moments of madness. I didn't care what they did to me, even when the knock on the door happened and my mum shouted for me to come to the door. I slowly walked down as if I didn't have a care in the world.

"Beverley, the police are here." My mum shouted all surprised.

"So?" I said in a rather calm and cold voice.

"They want to talk to you, what have you done?"

I thought I would say I did nothing, and then I just said nothing. I could now feel nerves building up inside me. I was now scared what was going to happen to me. I could feel my face blush and the tears build up in my eyes. The policeman was talking to me, but I didn't hear a word, the female police officer just ushered me to their waiting car. Before I knew I was in the police station, sitting in an interview room. I was left there to stew for a while. Every now and then someone would come in and ask if I was okay? Usually a WPC holding a cup of tea in a tin cup. Soon I had the duty solicitor in with me and basically, they knew who I was but didn't have a clue who the other three boys were. It was made clear that things would be a lot easier for me if I came clean and told them who they were.

I thought about it - the thought of doing time frightened the living daylights out of me. Here I was, a seventeen-year-old girl, scared out of her wits, not believing what I had done and now my future looked very bleak indeed. All my own fault of course. And just to put the cherry on the cake, I knew I was pregnant.

Tony was the father and I was now in the situation where I had to report him as my partner in crime to save my own neck. He did not know I was pregnant, I never told him, what with everything that happened to my dad I just was a mass of angry hormones. I was torn between the two. I had feelings for him, and he liked me, but we were young just living our lives as you do. The pregnancy was an accident and I wasn't sure how happy he would be about it. I wasn't even sure how I felt. Everything was happening at once and I just couldn't cope.

Soon I gave the boys up. The police officers left the room and I was placed into a cell to be transported to the magistrate's court in the morning. They called my mum for me and she brought me some clean clothes to wear for the hearing.

After another sleepless night, I was back in the police car being driven the court. I was then kept in another cell beneath the courts. I had a horrible shock when I recognised the boy's voices in the other cells. I didn't know how I could face them. I cried in the cell, yearning for my mum and dad to come and be with me but I knew it couldn't happen.

Soon the door opened, and a police officer escorted me up to the court. In the dock were the boys. They sat and faced forwards. They did not even look at me or acknowledge me. I couldn't blame them, they were only here because of me. If only I had not been so stupid, if only my dad never was arrested, if only I didn't get that gun, my world was full of if only. I so wanted to tell Tony I was carrying his baby, but clearly a dock in the court was not the best place to do it. Maybe once we were all outside I can tell him?

The proceeding started, the court deemed the crime to be too serious to be dealt with at the magistrates and was adjourned for a crown court hearing. This meant potentially we all could get more than a year inside prison. We got our court date and then there was the matter of bail. I was told there was a good chance of getting bail as they rarely placed girls of my age on remand. The details were discussed in court, just more words flying around the court room that I really was not taking in. Soon the magistrate made his announcement, we were all remanded in custody. I was shocked, I looked behind me into the public gallery and saw my mum crying. She watched me be led away first, the boys were kept separate from me and soon was alone in the cell beneath the court again. I just cried.

Soon I was at reception of Holloway Prison. Everything just seemed so loud, huge, gates clattered, and keys turned. Officers shouted orders down corridors which echoed around the area. It was miles away from my ideal Essex countryside.

I felt I could not breathe, the fresh air had disappeared and was replaced by a barrage of sound. Soon all my personal belongings were searched through, some I could keep, and others had to be placed in plastic see through bags and tags tied around the top. I signed my life away on loads of forms and soon I was led to my dorm.

Chapter 6 – Bang Clang Bang Clang.

It seemed to me that no matter what time of day it was, a security gate was being unlocked, opened, slammed closed and locked. The sound of the metal keys turning in their locks, piercing bang as the door was slammed shut, the turn of lock clunking back and then the jingle of keys being hooked back on the Prison officers belt. The noise seemed to echo from everywhere. During the night you could hear shouting, or crying or sporadic laughter. It was eerie, the corridors of the prison seemed to go on for miles. Sounds bouncing off the painted walls, each sound made by a woman locked up in her own cell. I was placed in a dormitory. It looked more like an army barracks, beds covered with scratchy blankets, white sheets on the bed beneath and the flattest pillow you would have ever seen in your life.

In my dorm were ten beds, five either side of the room. At night at least one of the women locked up here were crying or having bad dreams. A few times it would be me, I did not have a clue how long I would be locked up in there. I had a 3 week wait until my Crown court appearance and then after that, who knows? I was an armed robber, the thought of going home and seeing my family again soon seemed remote. I felt unwell when I entered the prison, but I thought it was nerves or anxiety. I longed for my mum and my dad. My dad was in a prison in Gloucester and here was his daughter banged up in Holloway. What a family people must have thought we were.

Before I had time to get used to the prison routine I found myself in pain in my abdomen. I was able to go to the toilet, where I saw blood between my legs. As the pain increased, the blood flow became heavier and soon I was close to passing out. I must have called out, as soon there was shouting and arms going around me to lift me from the floor. Soon it was a blur, just flashing lights, distorted voices and a complete feeling of helplessness.

Soon I was aware of being in clean clothes, a new bed with crisp white sheets and a Prison Officer sitting next to me. I had been rushed to hospital and even in my terrible physical and mental state I could tell I was no longer prison. It was quiet, you could hear the footsteps of nurses on the tiled floor, no keys jangling and slamming of big metal gates. The prison officer, still wearing her uniform hat reached forward and took my hand.

"How are you feeling Beverly?" I didn't say a thing, I was still in a weak state. Soon more nurses came and went. I drank some water and slowly I started to feel more human. Soon a doctor came and told me I had lost my baby. It was five months old. The baby was a little girl. In the same sentence I was told I would feel some more discomfort and would have a little more discharge but other than that I would be fit to return to prison. Though I got sympathetic looks from everyone, they really did not think how it would affect me. I was in shock. It was the strain of trying to lift that bloody safe. I felt it was karma, I was stupid enough to do what I did, and I had to pay for it some way. I did something so stupid and soon after I paid the price. My baby was taken from me.

Soon I was heading back to Holloway in a car and before I knew it I was under my itchy blanket with the sheet pulled over my head crying. I never told Tony that I was having the baby. I knew, but guys of that age would not have received that sort of news well. I always waited for the right time, but it never came. Soon I was wrapped up in my own world, my father being arrested and whisked away to jail and all I focused on was trying to hurt the world that took him from me. Now Tony need never know I carried his daughter for five months, I was pretty sure that after coming clean to the police he would want nothing to do with me anymore anyway. It still hurt. I wish I told him, maybe he would have talked me out of doing something so stupid. In all honesty, I don't think he could if he tried. It was Karma.

Over the coming weeks as I awaited my court appearance, I was looked after well by the prison officers. They knew that this little frightened kid was not a horrible armed robber, despite my stupid actions. I was vulnerable, and frightened of what sentence I was going to get. My solicitor had told me that he had contacted all my family and asked them to come to the court in Chelmsford. I doubt he had to ask them as I know they would be there for me. However, he wanted them to speak up for me, tell the court I was not this criminal and basically, I had gone off the rails for personal reasons. I was not confident that this would work. I carried a shotgun around with me, it was loaded. Would I have pulled that trigger if need be? I can't say I would not have. My state of mind was in such turmoil, I just wanted to hurt someone, make them pay.

As I lay on my bed in the dorm, I could still feel the weight of the gun. What if it went off accidently? I could have killed myself, the boys or anyone. It sat loaded in the foot well, moving all over the place as I sped through country lanes and motorways. What was I thinking? Maybe I deserved time in prison, losing my baby girl maybe was not enough. All these thoughts went around and round in my head morning, noon and night.

Even during my communal times at meals and exercise, I felt I did not deserve anything good to happen to me. I was ashamed. I had so much time to think what could have happened I almost convinced myself I had shot someone. I could feel the weight of the gun, the smell of the polish, the power that radiated from it as I believed I was invincible. I believed no one could stop me. How can a piece of metal and a box of cartridges full of shot make you feel like that? It was as if I felt I had an invisible shield that no one could possible break through. I had three boys that would do anything I wanted, I could manipulate them as I wished. Three normal boys who had done no one any harm, soon they became robbers purely because I told them too. A little blonde girl with a shot gun.

Thank God, I did not kill anyone.

Chapter 7 - Crown Court.

My court date finally arrived. It seemed to take forever. I had already pleaded guilty in the magistrate court and now was awaiting sentence in the crown court. Due to my early plea of guilty, the boys had no choice but to plead guilty also. They were not happy with me at all, I was advised not to make eye contact as we would all be in the dock together. This was impossible, I so wanted to tell Tony that I had just lost his baby, I felt he had to know. I so wanted to write a letter and explain everything. I didn't want him to hate me, or the other boys for that matter. In my moment of madness, I had lost my boyfriend and his friends.

I tried to make sense of it all as I lay wide awake on my bed. Time seemed to stand still at night. A big clock high up on the dormitory wall ticked. It was like torture, it seemed to get slower and slower the longer I was in there. At night, it seemed to echo across the room. Some nights I watched it until the lights came on and it was time to get out of bed and prepare for yet another day banged up.

My court day was different. I was told to pack all my possessions into a big plastic bag and everything I owned was thrown across the floor near other bags owned by girls going to their court dates. The only way anyone knew whose was whose was by a big tag on top of the bag with a long number on it. I signed a sheet saying I was happy everything was packed. I didn't know why, I asked an officer and she told me it was in case I was freed. I could not see this happening. I got into the car and we drove through North London, then

East London and then out to the familiar Essex country side to Chelmsford County Court. Here my future would be decided. I wondered how many years I would get, how much more time could I really spend on that lumpy bed, listening to the sounds of the night and that God-awful clock.

We arrived at the court and again I found myself in another cell with several other ladies. We didn't really chat, just looked at the floor in a waiting pose. When you go through the justice system, you are forever waiting. Waiting for lights out, lights on, Breakfast, Lunch, Dinner, Court Dates, Solicitor visits, Family visits and the list goes on. The bits in between, the waiting time, is just dead time. Sitting pretending to be strong, wondering what is going outside. Even though it was only a few weeks you soon realise that those moments help you get through the day and before you know it, it starts all over again the next day. My Barrister came to talk to me before the appearance and told me that all my family had turned up. Both little nan and Grandad, big Nan and Grandad and of course my Mum. I so wanted to be with my Mum but also dreaded her seeing me like this. I was also warned that the boys would be walked up with me. Again, I had mixed feelings, it may be my only chance to tell Tony about our baby. It played on my mind ever since she left us. I didn't really care where I would end up, I believed it was karma. I took a gun and robbed garages and my baby was taken from me and now I would have to face Tony knowing that he hates me. After all, not only did I lead them down this path I also told the police. I was told to plead guilty and try to look remorseful as I did so. I was no longer this trigger happy little girl, striking out at the world because of her father. I was a stupid common criminal who believed she was about to lose everything that was good in her life.

I was marched up to court with the boys being escorted behind me. They didn't say a word, I just heard their steps echo through the corridors and up the stairway into the court. We sat in the dock and I could almost feel Tony sitting next to me. I turned my head ever so slightly and I could see that he was facing forward and not trying to make eye contact with me at all. The Judge came in and we stood. After confirming our names and address we were asked how we pleaded. Each in turn we said "guilty."

One by one our Barristers made a case to be lenient in sentencing. The boys had no previous criminal records, neither did I, so should count for something. Then my Barrister said that were some people here who wished to make statements to the courts and me. One by one my family were led into the witness box and made to swear the oath. My nans in tears as they told the court what a good hardworking girl I am, and this would never have happened if my Dad hadn't gone to prison. My Mum told the court how I doted on my Dad and even though he was a rough diamond, we had a very close relationship. They said how I worked for him at the garage, taking money and pumping petrol for customers. I was always on time and did a great job and everything that happened was totally out of character and it would never happen again.

After waiting in a holding cell for what seemed an eternity, we were marched back to the dock and told to stand. In turn each one of the boys got 5 years. I could hear their breathing get faster and faster as the realisation was sinking in. I waited to see if one of them would shout abuse at me, or even try to throw a punch but nothing. Then it was my turn. I clenched my fists and held my breath, I held back tears for as long as I could when it was announced I would receive two years of probation. At first, I thought it was 2 years in prison. I swallowed and stood there stiff as a board. I heard 2 years and nothing else. As we were marched back down to the cells, the boys were marched back to their cells and I was placed on a bench. The officer behind the reception bench, told me as soon as he had the court paper work sent down to him he would release me to probation and then I was free to go.

Free to go? I was going home? I could not believe it. I sat there with my huge bag of belongings I had accumulated while inside the prison awaiting to be interviewed by a probation officer. Soon a rather clumpy woman in sandals, a long flowing dress and a scarf around her neck ran in. She sat next to me and said," Are these details correct?" I looked, and it was my full name and address with a description of my offences. She then said, "Good, we will write to you for your first appointment." Got up and left, returning to court. Soon I was leaving the cell area. I walked towards the exit and the door was unlocked, as it opened I turned and looked back down towards the cell area. I knew the boys were in there, I felt for them. I was ushered out the huge doors and heard it slam behind me for the last time. If only we could have talked.

Chapter 8 - Maternity Ward

I met with my probation officer and agreed I would have to do some sort of work to pay back society. This work would at first be like a torture for me. I was placed into Orsett Hospital Maternity Ward. I was very nervous on my first day, I had to collect my uniform from the stores, it was a blue dress with a white apron and a little white hat. I also had a rather fetching cape that was red and blue. Once I had my neatly pressed uniform on I had to report for duties. One of my first tasks was to bathe new born babies. The little baby laid there looking like all the other babies in ward. I imagined if my baby would have looked like them. Every little cry reminded me of what should have been, it was like a dagger through heart each time I heard it. Soon I would have him or her wrapped up in big fluffy white towels drying them off and applying their nice fresh nappy with massive safety pin to hold it all in place. I also had to help mothers with breast feeding. There was a lot of pressure to breast feed and when it did not happen many women felt like they were somewhat failures. Most were still in physical shock after the birth and needed to relax and have an understanding ear to hear their worries, and that ear would sometimes be me. Some would have to go to the bottle, but most would successfully be able to breast feed their babies naturally. It was such a relief for the mother.

As well as being a good listener I would also have to help the mothers-to-be with administration, make them nice cups of tea and any other help they may require. I soon fell into the work and began to enjoy myself. As I walked about my duties I saw ladies waddling along the corridors almost fit to burst. It was difficult for me to watch them walk to their examinations and not wish that was me. I wanted to be one of the ladies holding their backs, groaning and moaning as they walked in and was laid out on their beds. It just was not to be. Not a day went by when I didn't think of her, even to this day.

The Outpatients' clinic was far more exciting to watch. Women of all shapes and sizes waiting in the waiting rooms all holding their bottles of urine. Some in jam jars and others in milk bottles, they clutched them like their life depended on it. Soon the harsh Matron would come in the room and shout out, "Remove all clothing from the waist down please ladies, help us smooth things along." The mums to be in skirts with tights and knickers were fine, they just whipped the off and sat there rolling the under garments in balls and placing them in their hand bags. The ladies wearing trousers were mortified, they would look around hoping there was somewhere for them to get changed, but when they realised there was nowhere, they sheepishly removed them, laying the trousers over their laps and planting their handbags securely on top.

From what I could make out their examinations were no better. A cold heartless male Doctor, not even making eye contact before sliding his gloved fingers inside her. Making comments to his nurse to write down and then the poor lady ushered out the door now clasping an empty jam jar. It all seemed a bit harsh. There was lots of love for the babies as they screamed when hungry or needed a nappy change. They would be wheeled around the wards back and forth to their mothers, who were laying in their beds, pale as their sheets trying to get their strength back after the stressful birth.

Visiting time could be hectic with families all wanting to see the babies, but the rather large and loud Matron would be strict, only allowing two in at a time so the rest of the disgruntled family would be waiting in the waiting room comparing Matron to a Nazi and other rather rude comments. I was like a little ghost weaving in and out of the people, collecting food trays, dropped packets of cigarettes left on the waiting room floor. No one noticed me, as I looked at the babies wishing that could have been me. As I picked up the metal rubbish bins I could feel the cold metal of that bloody safe that we could not open on that fatal night.

Each night I would go home to my mum and discuss the day at the hospital, she could see in my face I was not right. Losing my baby girl because of a totally stupid few days of madness was eating me up inside. All I could think about was what might have been. I had pictures of her in my mind of what she would look like and each time I thought of her the pain was so hard to deal with.

Though you never forget, I had to move on and started to enjoy my work at the maternity ward. I got to know other nurses and orderlies and soon we would be having and tea together on our breaks and chatting about life. There was almost a class structure in the hospital, us the lowest level, then the nurses and then matrons and Doctors. We would see them pacing about from patient to patient filling in their clipboards at the end of their beds. Taking blood pressure and checking if the baby and the mother was taking to breast feeding. I would make sure I would keep my ward clean and tidy, hand out breakfast, lunch and tea. It was just as important. The ladies were far more pleased to see me with tea and biscuits than a nurse wielding a cold stethoscope.

Soon I worked my way into the maternity ward itself. I was helping in C sections, counting in and out the swabs and disposing of them afterwards. I would see little wrinkled alien like creatures make their entrances into the world, usually being held by a Midwife by the heel and being forced to scream to clear their tiny little lungs. Soon they would be wiped, weighed wrapped up and handed to mum to look at and then placed into their own little cot. There was none of this family with camcorders standing around the bottom of the bed and sweaty fathers trying not to faint at first sight of blood. All very business-like, the Father saw the baby and mother when it was deemed suitable and that was decided by the Matron. If you got on the wrong side of her life could be miserable. She may have been strict, but the wards were clean and ran like clockwork.

Soon I started to make some friends and I was whisked off my feet by a rather handsome tall man called Fred. Fred worked as a porter and we would see each other a lot as he would wheel the ladies to and from the delivery room. He was funny and made me laugh and smile, something I had not done for some time. Soon I was smitten. He took me out for drinks in the local pub and before I knew it I was not thinking about babies, I was thinking about fun, having a life and enjoying myself. Soon we were driving around the country lanes of Essex in my Mini having a wonderful time.

Suddenly, shock horror, Fred asked me to marry him. I could not believe it. I was so stunned I did not know what to say. My mouth opened but no words would come out. His big blue piercing eyes stared at me as he awaited my response, I said, "YES." He grabbed and picked me up hugging me and spinning me around like a rag doll. I could not believe this was happening, I was totally overwhelmed. I had hardly got to know him. After all the bad things that had happened to me this, I thought, would be a good thing. A new start with a new man. It could be just the tonic I needed. My feet were slammed back to Earth when I drove home and then realised I would have to tell my Mum.

Chapter 9 - The Blushing Bride.

My Mum was not very happy about my up and coming wedding. She tried to talk me out of it saying I was far too young to get married. I think deep down she wanted me to have a bit of a life before settling down. She had a distrust about men, she had formed her own independent life and relied on no man. I was 18 years old, on probation with just a Mini Van to my name. Fred was a Hospital Porter, though a worthy job, it did not bode well financially for my future. When I was little in 1950s, my Dad drove us to Switzerland for a holiday. It was one of the most beautiful experiences of my life. My Mum and Dad had worked hard for that, to buy the car, petrol and the hotels. It was not the sort of thing anyone really did in that time. My Mum wanted the best for me, a man that would take me away, whisk me off my feet and give me a great life and as far as she was concerned Fred was not that man. I, of course, would not listen. I was with Fred on the rebound from Tony and believed I was in love. It just felt so good that a good-looking man would want to be with me after all that horrid time I went through. I really could see nothing going wrong, I was happy as was Fred. I was excited and felt this was the right decision to make.

A June Wedding was planned to be performed in Grays Registry Office. My Mum, despite her objections to the whole event, did all the food and we had the reception back at her bungalow. The wedding went by in a blink of an eye. I had the most beautiful dress and a wonderful bouquet of white lilies. I was so swept away with the moment that it never occurred to me that Fred had no family or friends there. I didn't care, it was our day and all I wanted was a special day. Soon we were back at my Mum's bungalow with family and friends enjoying the celebrations. My Mum agreed we could stay there until we were able to find our own place and soon we were laying in our marital bed as Husband & Wife. I was so happy.

It did not take a long time for things to slowly go downhill. We were both still working at the hospital and soon his personality changed. He hated me talking to other men which I had to do at work, especially the Doctors. One night we were home, and he questioned me about someone I spoke to at work, I made the mistake of dismissing what he said as being silly and he slapped me. I had never been hit by a man before. I was in shock. We had barely been married a few days and now he is being violent towards me. I could not believe it, his character almost changed the day after we got married. He was always so happy before, it's what I liked about him the most, he always seemed so much fun. Now his face had changed, those dashing good looks were always looking stern and angry. Soon he barely grunted let alone talked to me, it was so scary.

Soon he hit me again and then again and soon after he tried to take a knife to me. I really had no idea why he was like this. I always remember one day I was driving Fred, his sister and her husband to the Cat Cracker Pub in Stanford le Hope. We were going along all nicely and then Fred smacked me across the face with the back of his hand for no reason. I was in so much pain I had to pull over onto the hard shoulder. A huge row erupted and soon we headed home and yet another night had been ruined.

There was a switch inside him that seemed to switch from a lovely happy go lucky fella to a complete violent maniac. I really was not doing anything wrong. I was so happy when we were together at the start. We seemed to have settled down nicely in my Mum's bungalow despite her initial objections and then after just six weeks of marriage my Mum and I had to kick him out. Why did it happen? I was distraught, I was scared to go to work but thankfully Fred had disappeared from work. Until one day he returned to my Mum's house and took a sledge hammer to my pride and joy, my Mini Van. He smashed it to pieces. If that was not bad enough, he did this in front of my Nan and Grandad, they were so shocked. We called the police and soon he was taken away. We heard that he had been released and a solicitor friend of the family told me to go to their house as they could not guarantee that he would not come back to do anything worse. I was petrified to go out, I was always looking over my shoulder just in case.

Soon afterwards we heard a commotion over the golf course near our home. We ran over and there was Fred driving a Mini over the greens and fairways of the course. All the grass was churning up under the tyres. He had his head out of the window and shouted out, "Like your new car?" Again, the police were called, I became so frightened, I was anxious and really became scared to leave the home. It had turned out that Fred had stolen the Mini somewhere and in his mind, he was making amends for what he had done to my own car. It took a lot of time to regain my confidence to return to normal life, but the memory of the violence was always with me. I believe to this day that it was karma for what I did to those poor people in those garages. I lost my baby and unknowingly married an unpredictable violent man.

Soon after I was approached by Fred's Mother and she asked me if he continued to take his medication after we moved in together? I was shocked, and did not even know he had to take any. It turned out that he was a schizophrenic and no one I knew who knew him had a clue. Why did he stop taking the meds? I really do not know.

Years later I heard he was imprisoned for a violent crime somewhere in the West Country. When I had moved away many years later, a man turned up at Mum's bungalow and introduced himself as, "Fred the man who married your daughter." He looked completely different, he had aged badly and was in obvious ill health. Mum said she did not know where I was and said her goodbyes and that was the last I heard of my first husband.

Chapter 10 – Beauty Queen.

It was suggested to me to apply for the Beauty Pageant that was held called Miss Valentine. I felt it was time after all my troubles with prison and Fred to let my hair down. This was something I definitely needed to do. My marriage had been dissolved and I felt confident that Fred would no longer try to harass me.

Soon the competition started, a group of us girls, about 25 or so, paraded in front of the judges in our beautiful dresses many of them were handmade as was the fashion at that time. I wore a short gold flecked dress and my blonde hair was cut really short. One by one they whittled us down to a handful and soon I was in the frame for a prize. I still did not believe I had a chance. Most of these young girls were whiter than white, butter would not melt in their mouths. I was a convicted armed robber, lost a baby to a convicted armed robber, got married and then divorced a maniac. So, I really did not take it too seriously I really was only there for a laugh and a pick me up. I just wanted to feel like the teenage girl I was before I saw my Dad taken away to prison.

Soon the competition was down to the last three girls. I was one of them. This meant I definitely would win something. I had the biggest smile across my face, I felt like a million dollars. All the positive attention I was getting made me feel like a normal person again. Then, shock horror it was announced that I, yes me, had won Miss Valentines. I could not believe it. There were photographers there all trying to get the best shots of me as I stood there with my sash and huge smile. I really had not even imagined what winning meant. I was soon asked to enter the Corringham Carnival Queen. This was even a bigger deal in the local community. I felt a lot more confident this time. I wore my brown mini dress with a white collar and kept my fingers crossed. There were to be three prizes, the Winner would be Carnival Queen and then two Princesses.

A Carnival Queen competition was very popular in those days, huge crowds would clap and cheer as you said your little speech on stage, explaining why you wanted to be Queen. I said I wanted to be Queen, so I could help with all the charity work that was involved and I enjoyed meeting new people. I then handed the microphone back, walked up and down the stage and twirled. Just a few months before the thought of doing this would have frightened the living daylights out of me, but I just felt so good now.

Soon the winners were announced, and I was crowned Princess. A young lady called Gabriella was crowned the Queen and Cathy was the other Princess. We were all so happy. From prison to princess in a year, who would have thought it? Soon more and photographers were taking our pictures for the local newspapers and all a sudden, I felt like a celebrity. It was wonderful. Just down the road from us was a huge shoe factory called Bata, they made all the fashionable shoes of the day and were very well known. They sent someone with lots of shoes for us to try and wear for our year of charity work. It was great publicity for Bata, as the Queen and Princesses of Corringham wore their latest designs and for us it was great as we kept them. Soon we were guests at all the local carnivals. We had our own float and would get great cheers as we moved through the high streets of various towns in Essex. It was wonderful escapism from the daily lives we all had, going to work scraping a few pennies together to go out and have a good night out. But this was Carnival, they were much more popular then than now. No one really sat in front of the television for hours at a time, we all got out and about. So, when the whole community had a good reason to join together for some fun, they did so in their droves. Each little village or town would have their carnival through the summer months. Dates were arranged so they did not clash with other carnival. Soon the Queen and Princesses were opening the carnivals themselves. We would cut ribbons and declare events, "Well and truly open." We even had the opportunity to open new supermarkets which were springing up all over the place at the time. It truly was a wonderful exciting time. Fred, Tony and the boys and Holloway prison soon became a long distant memory for me. I used to look forward to every weekend when I would dress up and be Princess for the day.

 I became so happy and relaxed I also started flirting with guys who liked the way I looked. The attention was wonderful, they did not see my past just who I was at that point. This led to me chatting to a handsome young man called Trevor who clearly liked me. He was a guitarist in one of the performing bands. He had a certain well-rehearsed swagger and he knew how to charm the birds out of the trees. We had drinks and before I knew it I had fell for the charm and soon we somewhere private ripping each other's clothes off.

Soon we said our goodbyes and I left with a skip in my step. I felt so good, I was more or less who I was before all the nonsense in my life had started. More carnivals came and went, more waving, smiling and being chatted up by various men in the crowds. I had suddenly become addicted to getting attention. It was all good, I was noticed more, not just when I was on stage or opening another supermarket but when I was out and about. I was smiling more, I felt so confident I felt like I could take on the world. I was happy, really happy. My Mum and I got on well back at her bungalow. I would help with her kennels, see my friends and perform my charity work at weekends. What could go wrong?

As the chill of autumn approached, I found out I was pregnant. I had a little bump and the fear of what happened before filled me with dread. At one of the charity events I was wearing a very beautiful long dress and in the photographs, you can just see the small bump. I had such mixed feelings, thankfully I had a mother that supported me, and I knew she would help me no matter what. I felt karma was smacking me in the face again. Each time I started to have more fun a huge event would happen and put me back in my place. I was determined not to let anything bad happen to this baby.

It was during this funny period of being pregnant and still a carnival princess that I met Jeff. We got on really well and started dating. I broke the news to him that I was already pregnant, and he broke the news to me that he was married and, so we started a relationship. His marriage was not at its best and he was all fine about me being pregnant.

Soon the carnivals were no more, and I was at the bungalow resting, as the bump got bigger and bigger I did less and less. I still walked about the kennels and did chores around the home, but I made sure I did nothing too stressful to my body. With support from Jeff and my mum everything seemed to be going smoothly.

As my waters broke, I got word to Trevor to tell him his baby was going to be born and soon I was sitting in the maternity ward with my healthy boy in my arms, Jason. He was beautiful, and I was so happy. On a beautiful August summer day one of the best things ever to happen to me did so. Jeff and Trevor were both there, it was all fine and everyone was happy. A new chapter was starting I my life and I was over the moon.

Chapter 11 – New men in my Life.

It was well known by all around us that Jeff was not Jason's father. People would ask if he was ok with this, bringing up another man's child but he really was. Trevor, Jason's biological father, disappeared soon after the birth and never saw Jason until he was five. Jeff had a baby girl who was about fifteen months old when Jason was born and though his marriage was clearly on the rocks, his wife Sue and I became good friends. We are still friends till this very day.

The three of us moved into my bungalow where the kennels were and set up a nice little home life. I worked at the kennels when needed. It was a seasonal business, so only busy during the holiday periods. Jeff was working as a delivery driver, transporting vegetables from the farms up to the London markets. Though things were ticking over nicely we decided to try increase our income by setting up a car valeting business. We could do this at the bungalow as we had a lot of ground to park the cars. We were helped by a very suave and charming man called John Adair. He was a second-hand car dealer and had lots of contacts in the motor world and would kindly put business our way.

From the money we made and some additional loans and credit we decided to rent a garage. It may seem like a strange thing to do, especially after my history with them. However, I did know the business well and knew how to make them work. I also learnt a lot of good things from dad when he worked at them and it stuck. I didn't want to keep looking back, I was looking forward and this would be a positive move for both of us to make. Though Jeff was working, he was still very lazy, he had no get up and go. I thought setting up our own business would be good for us. The harder we worked the more we could earn, and we could have a great life, all three of us.

The garage we rented was in Grays. We got it all set up and with the help of a few contacts like John Adair we started to make some money. I would leave Jeff there on days I was needed at the kennels and everything went along nicely. Until I had another shock to the system. I was pregnant. After everything going so well with Jason, I was actually very happy. With two incomes and a stable home I thought this would be a wonderful addition to our family home. Though our relationship was not perfect, Jeff was pleased and supportive.

When I was four months pregnant I felt something was not right. Before I knew it, I was in Orsett Hospital, being completely checked over. Blood test after blood test, blood pressure and examinations. I was scared, I could not go through another loss like before in Holloway. I laid in the bed with family around me and awaited the news.

After some time, a Doctor announced to us that I had indeed lost my baby. A baby girl. No reason was given, it was as if having a daughter was not meant to be. I cried in the bed and felt my Mum's arms around me. I felt like a failure, I was not sure if this was karma again, what had I done to deserve this? What has that poor baby girl done to deserve this?

Over the coming days I really could not function. I was quiet and not my usual bubbly self. I distanced myself from Jeff and focused more on the kennels than the garage. The few days I did go to the garage I struck a friendlier relationship with John Adair. He spoke to me differently than the way Jeff did. He was more upbeat, very flirty and knew how to make a woman feel good about herself. I really needed that at the time. I knew he was married and I knew he was a womaniser, but it didn't matter, I fell for him. Soon I was having a casual affair with him behind Jeff's back and I really enjoyed it. We never dated as in went to restaurants or things like that. We just met for sex. I loved being with him and when it was over for that night or day I went back to my life at the kennels as if nothing had happened. I knew it was wrong but then he made me happy and I did not really care. It became apparent that Jeff was becoming even more lazy than usual. We were getting chasing letters from suppliers and the banks about outstanding loads and rent to pay. He was just not on top of anything. I went there to try and clear up the mess but after a while it was clear his heart was not in it. Just like my heart was not in the relationship, I decided not to throw any more money at the garage and we gave it up.

I saw John a lot more, I had no reason to see him other than to be together behind Jeff's back. When I was with him I felt very special, he made me feel like life was worth living and I should live in the moment. Of course. he wanted sex, but the feeling was mutual. At home, Jeff seemed to bum around from one job to another. We were together but no spark. I guess it was laziness on both our parts or we were just stuck in a rut that we felt we could not get out of, but neither of us tried to make our home life any better. He was good with Jason and did his own thing. I think we both had it too easy, a roof over our heads, a bed with regular income. Neither of us wanted to rock the boat.

Soon I was discovered that I was pregnant again. I was struck down with fear, I could not go through another loss again. I wasn't really in love with Jeff anymore and John not in a situation to start a new family I felt incredibly alone. I knew I was silly, but I got caught up in the moment, again this was the Karma machine working, being unfaithful and not focusing on my family. That is how I thought at the time. My roller coaster life gave me lots of highs of which I paid with the equal amount of lows. Each time I felt things were going smoothly there would always be a bump in the road. I almost got to a point where I could never believe I would be happy or enjoy my life.

That was until my son Joe was born. I held him for the first time and knew it was right. He was healthy and a screaming bundle of wee and poo and that made me very happy. I remembered all that time I worked at Orsett Hospital wishing those screaming bundles of joy could be mine, and here I was with my second boy. I felt very happy despite my circumstances, and the love I had for my boys kept me going.

Jeff assumed Joe was his son, but I knew he wasn't. He was John's son, but I did not have the heart to tell him. John never knew he was his either, again I was keeping everything smooth at home, so we could all have a nice happy house hold. All I wanted was a nice home to bring my boys up in.

They were the most important thing in my life and I worked hard to give them the same love that I had growing up from my Mum.

I knew it would be difficult with the extra mouth to feed. My Mum offered to look after them both when needed so I could get another job. In those days, you could walk out of one job and straight to another if you were not too fussy and just needed wages to live and support your family. That is all I wanted to do. Just help us get by. I needed some time where nothing went wrong, the boys could thrive and we all be happy living in the Essex countryside.

I soon managed to get a job at a company called Euro Met. It was a metal fabrication company, there were plenty of staff and I fitted well there working in the administration part of the factory. There were rumours going around that the place was not doing so well, and it may be short lived, but I wasn't too bothered by this, I needed this job to keep me going until I found something better. One thing for sure is that if there are men around, I will no doubt fall for someone and I did. His name was Mick. He worked as an estimator, was always in a suit and was quite good looking. I decided to let my guard down again and live a little.

Not long before my Mum had sold her business and her bungalow to my Aunty Cheryl. She moved in with her husband and daughter and started to take over the business. My Mum moved to a mobile home on the grounds leaving the other bungalow for me. It all seemed to be working out very well. My Mum was very generous as she felt I should get something from the sale of the business as I had worked so hard on it as well and gave me £20,000. I was gob smacked, it was a huge amount of money, I played safe and just put it in the bank.

As more rumours flew around Euro Met about its demise, Mick told me how he was worried about losing his job and wish he could find money to invest in the company. Then I got soft and greedy. I felt for him and all the staff there, I enjoyed being there and did not want to see the place go under. I told Mick I had a lump sum in the bank and he then began telling me how much money I could make as an investor in the company. The figures he mentioned sent me giddy and the greed gene I clearly had inherited from my Dad clicked in. I gave him the £20,000 to invest in the company.

It was at this point that Jeff and I split up. Jeff had met a lady called Ann and he was seeing her while I was seeing Mick. It was apparent that our time had run its course and it was the right time to call it a day. The problem was that Jeff was not going to leave easily. He barricaded himself the bungalow and demanded a payoff of £5,000 to leave. I could not believe this, I felt I had given him enough in life and the fact that he was too lazy to make anything from it was his own fault. As usual I did the easy thing, and paid him. I resented every single penny, but after all these years I just wanted him gone. Joe was now ten years old and the wasted years with him just seemed to fly by with nothing actually happening, it was sad.

I regained access to the bungalow and he had completely trashed it. It was disgusting. Furniture was broken, pipes and fittings broken. I could not believe that after more than ten years he would destroy our family home. He moved away with an animal welfare officer called Ann and ended up living in Wales. This meant that Mick and I become more of an item, which certainly suited me. It was nice to be in a relationship and not worry about being seen or getting caught out somewhere.

Time went on and I thought that I should be getting some return on my investment, but I got nothing. Mick and I argued, I told him how he had fed me bullshit and like an idiot I fell for it. He assured me I would get my money back and more, I just had to hold tight. Every day I turned up for work I was still hearing that the company was on its last legs and it was only a matter of time before the receivers came in. I again accused Mick of screwing me over and he knew how unhappy I felt.

It was then he came up with a plan. He talked me into creating a fake member of staff and claiming his wages. I could do this as I worked in the appropriate department. I had the blinkers on again. I knew it was illegal but all I wanted was my money back. I signed the cheques and soon we were cashing them. At the time I had no sense of wrong doing, I was just sick and tired of being used and being too trusting. I wanted all my money back and that was all I cared about. Needless to say, any company that is going into receivership will be having its accounts and cash flow scrutinised and unbeknown to us the Police were called to investigate, and we got caught.

Chapter 12 - Back in Prison.

I felt so stupid. Influenced by another man who would make me do something I knew was wrong and I knew there was a possibility I would go to prison. I so wanted to get my savings back, I really believed that once I had the money safely back in my bank life would go on as normal. It was sold to me as a "What can go wrong?" sort of thing and I fell for it. Again, I felt the karma machine was churning out its just deserts again. I left court in a van and was shipped off to Bullwood Hall Prison. Bullwood was once seen as a modern prison for female young offenders and then slowly over time as other prisons became full it started to take adult females. In many ways it was worse than Holloway Prison. You still had to slop out, I was locked away in a single cell for hours at a time. You were only allowed two showers a week and because I was only in there a short time I was not given a great deal to do. It made the three months I was in there seem like three years. Even during the short time I was there, there were fights and attempted suicides. Girls were going off their heads inside there. I knew I had to try and keep it together, keep my head down and stay out of sight.

All the time alone in the cell gave me too much time to ponder my life and soon I felt as if my mood was slipping down into a dark depression. It was as if since my Dad went away to prison I needed some sort of substitute to make up for his absence. I knew I was smart enough to make it alone in my life, but being in a relationship was something I always liked and enjoyed. I just wasn't very good at picking the right partner. I was not sure if Mick and I would stick together but I knew in the future I would have to be a bit more independent in some ways and not so trusting.

After a few weeks I started a friendship with a lady in the prison called Pauline. She told me about working as a steward at various places like football clubs. It sounded like the ideal sort of work for me. She was released just before I was and when I got out we got in touch. Soon Mick was joining me at home. I decided to give it another go, but this time I would be more vigilant and make sure I think before I agree to anything.

Soon Mick and I had been put in touch with Old Owen Sports Club in Potters Bar, Hertfordshire. It came with a nice little two-bedroom bungalow and before we knew it we were settling in nicely in our new place. Initially once we moved and started working there I had my guard up, I did not want anything to ruin this. We had a great opportunity to have a nice honest life, meet new friends and give my two boys a great life also. Soon I was ordering catering supplies, running between the bar and the kitchen making sure everything was going well. My life had gone from sitting in a cell alone for hours on end to quite a hectic job. Keeping people happy and arranging entertainment for them, it was wonderful. Soon I was not even thinking about the past, I was making sure the bitter beer barrel had been changed, rotating food in the fridge, dealing with phone call after phone call. Making sure the boys were happy and doing well at school. It never ended.

After eighteen months of hard work at the sports club we were offered the chance to become stewards of Cruise Hill

Golf Club. As much as I loved what we were doing, I felt we needed a challenge, to step it up a bit. I wanted to show what I really could do. I loved using my catering skills and my newly found organisation skills. I had gained confidence in the role and felt I could take on a lot more. My two boys were happy also and even though it meant they would have to move to a new school they seemed quite happy. Mick agreed, this could be our chance to really thrive and finally have a good life.

Crews Hill Golf Course is in Enfield, so not a million miles from where we were. It was to be a live-in position and a lovely 3-bedroom house came with the job. The course was beautiful, and it had a wonderful club house that seemed huge compared to the last place. With such a wonderful back drop I would be able to show off my flair for good food and drink. We made the move and soon we were looking over the spectacular grounds of the course. The club house was much bigger, more staff, bigger events and many more customers. My day would start early in the morning with those that teed off first thing and finish late at night after the bar would close and the drinkers and diners had gone home. I would flop into bed at 2 am and then have to get up at 6am to get the whole process running again. I ran on adrenaline for six days a week. Then on Monday I would collapse on the sofa, read magazines and slob about while the boys were at school. It was relentless but also exciting and fun.

Things were going incredibly smoothly and we all seemed to be incredibly happy. Mick arranged the accounts and I dealt with the customers, we looked after the boys and everything seemed to be going well. One day as I lay on the sofa, coffee in one hand and magazines in the other, Mick set out the books on the table to go through. He had the normal pile or receipts, delivery notes and letters all piled up alongside him and then systematically he went through them one by one. As I lay there pretending to be Lady Muck for a few hours, I noticed out of the corner of my eye Mick constantly keep glancing at me as he worked on the accounts. At first, I thought it was him seeing if I was alright, but he looked a little bit shifty. I let this go on for a while and then realised he did not want me to see what he was doing. I got up and challenged him and he made out that everything was fine, and we were doing well. We should have been doing well, we had full capacity dining nearly every night, bar sales were through the roof and customers could not get enough of the place. So, I settled down and just assumed all was well and it was me being paranoid after everything that had happened in the past. It was natural I guess.

On one of my days off I decided to go and seem my Mum at the kennels. As ever she was busy getting the dogs food and drink sorted out after their long morning walks and the dogs yapped and barked away happily in the back ground. My Mum now lived in a caravan on the grounds after she gave her bungalow to me to live in. It would give us stability for the boy if the stewardship position did not work out. Also on the grounds was another bungalow and this belonged to my Aunty Cheryl. She had sold the business to Cheryl and they both worked on it together making it very profitable. It seemed we were all doing well.

I decided to go and check in at my place and see everything was ok. As I opened the door there was a pile of mail on the floor. I had expected this, I did not get the chance to get away from the golf course that often, so it had been a while since I had been there. I sat down thinking how the place could do with a hoover and a nice spring clean and then decided to go through the mail. There were a lot of letters from the bank. At first, I thought they were statements and then I had the shock of my life. They were demands to pay my mortgage for the bungalow. It was going to be reprocessed. I could not believe it. I felt sick to the stomach. I read more and more letters and soon it became apparent that Mick had not been paying the mortgage. I had taken my eye off the ball and trusted him yet again and here I am about to lose my home.

It turns out he was gambling. He was gambling big. He lost my savings with a scam and we paid for that and now he gambled my boys and life away. I could not believe it. I screamed and shouted at him, but it was going to change nothing. I worried about my boys as more change was going to affect their lives. Mick had screwed me over and soon I told him to leave and never come back. I wanted to put a knife in his chest I was so angry. How I didn't I really do not know. I walked away from the steward's job, something I absolutely loved, took my boys to my bungalow sat down and imploded. I just shut down, I could not function.

I lay in the spare bed with a duvet and blankets over my head. I wanted to the world to leave me alone. Once again, my past played before my eyes like a bad film and soon I plummeted into depression. I was physically and mentally broken. I really could not take anymore. I heard my Mum cooking the boys their dinners and putting them to bed and I was paralysed. I felt they were better off without me. I felt their life would be better for them if I was dead. My stupid decisions with men who I knew were even lazy or untrustworthy had ruined my life right from the day my Father was shipped off to prison. I felt like I would never have another man in my life, how could I trust again? What was I going to do now? All I knew was the dark place I was in seemed like the only place I could exist. I would close my eyes, see all my past again and again and soon enough I just shut down. I could not control my crying. The boys would try and come and see me, but I was too embarrassed to see them. I could not even bring myself to speak to my own beautiful boys. All they wanted was a cuddle, but I felt I was not good enough for them. My Mum seemed to be doing a good job, I could trust her. She was really the only person in my life I could trust. I knew where I stood with her and I always did. My depression deepened as I heard the boy's life go on without me. I didn't wash, brush my teeth and soon I was in that spiral of not caring for myself because of my low self-worth. I felt like a failure, I felt so stupid, I lay there and over and over again the faces of those who I allowed to screw my life up stared back at me laughing.

Just to add insult to injury I had to leave my beloved home. Cheryl's daughter, Tracey and son in law had bought my home preventing it from being reprocessed by the banks. This was all well and good but either way I had to go. I was in no fit state to arrange viewings and search for somewhere else.

In the end my Mum had found me a flat in Leigh on Sea. It was pokey, quiet and it was as if I was deleted from my family's world and shoved off to this rabbit hatch in an area that I did not know very well. For me it was another duvet to bury my head under and hope all the bad things that had plagued me would go away.

I wished I was dead.

Chapter 13 - Escaping to France.

As with most downs in my life I fought constantly to try and pick myself up and start over again. This time it just seemed like an impossible task. My boys were both out in the world starting their own lives. I was now single after being used again and as usual the only person who saw what was going on was my Mum. She knew I was not in a good place. At first, I was completely inconsolable, I would not eat, wash or even get out of bed. The duvet became my shell. No one could get through to me while I was under there. I had no concept of time, not even the worlds news penetrated the fabric. I was in my Bev capsule, locked away from everyone in the world, especially men. Even my Mum struggled to get sense through to me. Depression is an awful affliction. I tried to be strong for far too long and I just broke. I had lost all my confidence to be able to get back into the real world. I never tried to end it all, but if it happened and I could have been aware of it I would not minded one bit. Though my family were the most important things in the universe to me I felt like I was some sort of burden. I would have missed them more than my life itself but my desire to find happiness, or even normality in my life was a constant struggle that I could never achieve. If there was anyone who could get me out of my dark place it was Mum. She was the kick up the arse I really needed. As usual when I lost my confidence and felt as if the whole world was against me, my Mum was there. I felt as if she must have been sick and tired of seeing my ups and downs in life and always being the life jacket that saved me from the choppy sea of life. Even though I was too trusting or sometimes just stupid she never judged me. She knew I was just searching for happiness and a good life and sometimes I just tried too hard.

After several talks with my Mum, I moved the duvet off me and decided to try once again at rebuilding my life. I did not feel as if I really had the strength to do it, but what choice did I have. I could not live under the duvet on my bed forever I needed purpose, I needed to find something I was good at doing and not have to rely on anyone else to make a go at it.

Soon I was applying for jobs, ploughing through the local newspapers searching for anything. That did not help my depression either, most jobs I was either not qualified to apply for or just cleaning for a few hours here and there. I would have taken anything, but I really wanted to perform the sort of work I enjoyed and was good at. It was not long before I saw a catering franchise available at Benfleet Yacht Club. It looked like it would be a good way back into catering, not much pressure just good honest hard work. It was a small club with lovely members and the menu was simpler than I was used to. I had to supply the food and pay the rent for the kitchens but all the money that came in was for me and after all my outgoings I started to make a living. At first I had no money to buy the food, my Mum loaned me money for the first few weeks of shopping required and soon I was underway again. I enjoyed catering and loved meeting people, so I was always well suited to that sort of work. The menu was mainly sandwiches and snacks with some hot lunches but all easy enough for me to prepare and serve on my own. I did not need any staff and working alone suited me down to the ground. No one else to screw it up and no one else I must watch with the books and cash. It would all be down to myself. The harder I worked the more I made and happier all my customers were in the clubhouse.

The problem with not having staff was that I needed to be there from start to finish seven days a week. I did not mind this, I loved the work and soon my focus was finding my own place. Rent prices were rocketing and soon I realised I could only afford a one bedroom flat in Leigh on Sea. I got it through an agency and needed a month's money upfront and a month's money for a deposit. The place was like a rabbit hatch, but it was my own space and it was exactly what I needed to get myself away from the kennels that just seemed to be toxic to me now. As usual my Mum loaned me the money for the flat and soon I was sitting in an empty flat, planning menus and writing out shopping lists.

I stopped looking back and concentrated on my new life. Though I knew what I was doing I still lacked lots of confidence and felt incredibly fragile. I hated feeling weak, I felt as if I had been a total mug but letting these people ruin my life. I felt as if it ever happened again there would be no return from it, I would roll up into a little ball and hide away forever. All I kept thinking was I must never ever let it happen again.

The spring and summer months were incredibly busy for me. As the yacht owners came down to sit and pose on their boats while the tide was in. As I prepared the food in the mornings I could see the sun rise in the mouth of the Thames estuary and see it set in the West at night. It was all rather pleasant, there was always a nice atmosphere there and everyone was incredibly friendly.

Soon I seemed to catch the eye of a charming older gentleman called Bob. He had white hair, was attractive and somewhat of a charmer. We got chatting at the bar and soon I noticed him turning up in a Corvette, which was something you did not see every day. Soon he asked me out for spin in the car and before you knew it we were dating. He was open about the fact that he was married, but they had separate rooms and the marriage had been dead for some time. Of course, I did not know this, but we clicked so well I decided to accept this on face value. Soon I was not all work and no play and began enjoying life a bit more. We would go out for long drives in his car, and we would spend a lot of time having drinks at the yacht club.

Over a period of six months or so we had clearly become a couple. We saw each other lots, he spent nights at my flat and we were generally having a nice time. During this time, he started mentioning how he had land and a barn to convert in France. This all seemed very nice to me, a place to get away where we can enjoy wine and lovely food on the barns' patio and soak up some of the local culture. The more he told me about it the more interested I became. Two acres of land where we could become self-sufficient, growing our own crops, maybe live stock for milk, make cheese it all sounded rather perfect.

He would keep mentioning it in conversations and soon it was rather obvious that I wanted to go there. I could leave all my troubles behind and start afresh, it just sounded all too good to be true. It was not long before he asked me to go out with him, I was so pleased. I gave notice at the yacht club and did the same for my flat and soon I was packing my bags of the few things I had. I had told everyone of this wonderful life I was going to have. Needless to say, everyone was pleased for me. I even took my dog, he would love having all that space to run about and chase rabbits etc. I told everyone they could visit and to make sure to keep in touch, and just like that I said goodbye to my life in Essex.

So, we set off in his car, seat to ceiling of suitcases and one rather excited dog.

Soon we were arriving at a small village called Villequier. It is a lovely little village right on the River Seine, it all looked rather lovely. We then left the village and headed out a short while, soon we were driving up an unsealed road and opening an old gate to what looked like a field of nothing. As we moved further along I saw a tiny caravan and what looked like a pile of old bricks. I mean some of it was standing up right and there was what seemed to be a roof with no slates or tiles on it, but surely that could not be my dream barn conversion? It was.

The local area was quite beautiful, and our piece of land was the blot on the landscape. It was horrible, just a field, a pile of bricks and caravan that seemed to lean in the wind. There was not enough room in it to swing a cat. I closed my eyes and realised that I had done it again, I had allowed myself to be fooled again and I really did not know what to do. I should have told him to take me home and leave it as that, but I couldn't. I would have looked such an idiot. I fell for a charmer's stories again and I knew I had to pay. I would stay and make a go of it. The stubborn part of me was determined to make the life I had been dreaming of since I knew I was going to go to France. To feel my bubble pop the minute I got there was like a knife in the chest. I knew what people would think, I knew if I told them I would get those knowing looks, "Oh Bev you are so stupid, too trusting why don't you think these things through?" They would be right, but for once I was not going to give them the satisfaction.

There was no toilet, no proper heating except for layer upon layer of clothing. I used to feel like the Michelin Man in bed, I could hardly move my body at the joints I was so wrapped up. If the romance had not already left our relationship, it certainly did so when he asked me those immortal words all of us ladies long to hear.

"We need to dig a cess pit."

My enthusiasm for life nearly disappeared, I wanted to dig his grave and bury him, but I grabbed a spade and slowly we began to dig a deep hole for all our waste to drain to. As each clang of the spade hit the soil I imagined being in a small café drinking red wine and eating cheese and baguettes. I know it is a bit cliché, but this was the life I envisaged for us. I thought the barn would need me to make cushions and curtains, not actually build the whole bloody thing from the ground up.

As the hard slog continued I imagined where we could keep some chickens, grow our vegetables and even dreamt of baking our own bread. The kitchen took shape and was a tiny stove, we finally had a table and heating from a diesel burning heater. During the winter months the diesel would freeze so on came the layer upon layer of clothing to get through the days and horrible nights.

I hated being there, I had no real life and soon insisted we take in the local village and see what was around the village. The beautiful River Seine flowed past the town and the roads were quite empty no matter what time of day. It was so tranquil so different to home, but this was of course my home now. Apart from family I had no links to Essex, no home, no job, nothing. We wandered along the river bank and I wondered if I could really make this my home.

The constant being frozen to the bone was very depressing, but the lovely town and people that inhabited it gave me some hope that things could improve.

On our land were twelve apple trees and one pear tree and soon the autumn months meant they were full of fruit ready to be picked. Traditionally these apples were used for cider, but at first, we did not have a clue what to do. I mentioned this to a lady I had become friendly with in town and before I knew it about ten locals turned up at our land with huge sticks and bags. Within minutes they were bashing the hell out of the branches in the trees and the apples fell on the floor like hailstones. Myself and a couple of others had these huge sacks and we followed behind bagging all the apples up and moved them near the barn. We were told to get as many bottles as we could and after the tree bashing we approached the restaurants and hotels asking for bottles they no longer needed.

Soon I was elbow deep in fairy liquid washing all the bottles out, we had every type you could imagine, wine, beer and spirits and soon on the kitchen table they all stood there drying. Probably not the most hygienic thing to do, but it was for our own use, so we really did not mind.

A few days later a man with a huge press came to us. Every year this man would go to each home, farm, orchard and press the apples to make cider. Before you knew it, we had our apples being crushed and the lovely apple juice was flowing into barrels. The town had really come together for us, they showed us how to store them, bottle them and one of them took a few bottles away to make calvados for us. It was like rocket fuel but incredibly tasty. During those cold nights it was the only thing that got me through the night.

As we got into the normal routine of life at the barn, Bob decided he needed to take trips back to the UK to pick up things we could not get in France. He was going to go alone while I stayed there with my dog and looked after things. He said he would leave me some money and he would be back in a few days. Once I was alone, I decided to see how much I had to fend for myself and maybe get myself a nice bottle of wine and relax in front of the diesel heater like you do. He left me ten Euros. Yes, just ten bloody Euros to last me and the dog for what turned out to be a week.

I hated not having an income of my own, I hated being totally dependent on one man, a man who knew I had nothing in my own name and used it to have control over me. Soon he was making regular trips back and forth to the UK and you did not have to be a detective to realise that he must have been going back to his wife or seeing someone else. My problem was I was stuck in France, no money, no friends or family and nowhere to go. We had apple trees so made some cider and grew vegetables which was nice, but it really was not the life I thought I was going to have.

Soon I decided to take matters in my own hands and searched a way I could make my own money. I saw an advert for to be personal assistant for an elderly gentleman who just so happened to be English. He told me that he would love to have employed me but there was a law in France that you must offer work to French Citizens first before offering work to immigrants. Also, I did not have the correct paper work to gain employment in the first place. I needed to get a Carte De Sejour, which is basically my residence permit. Once I could get this I could then apply for work. I soon got chatting to other English people in the village and was told to speak to the owners of the Coach House Inn right on the river bank. I told them my situation and soon they were helping me with all my paperwork and once it came through they offered me a job, it was as a chamber maid, but it felt so good to finally know I could work for my own money. I had got to the point where I had so little when Bob went back to the UK I had to use food banks. I never thought I would be put in such a position, but I was so grateful for them at the time. You were given boxes of dried milk, tins of beans and rice. The basics to keep you going, it gave me enough energy to get a paid job where I could finally fend for myself.

Despite the barn being set up and the veg patch full of lovely crops to eat, I felt alone and vulnerable. I could feel my depression growing each day and despite the lovely friendships I had made there both French and English I was not happy. I missed my boys, I missed my Mum and other friends and family. Bob was clearly not committed to me and I had no security there. If he died everything would go to his wife and I would be left with nothing. All that hard work I had put in to it, the freezing cold nights and the days without food being stuck all alone in the barn that never ever seemed to be finished.

I don't think I would have lasted the four years if it was not for the kindness of the locals in the area, they really tried to take me under their wing and help me the best they could. After several conversations on the telephone with my Mum, she told me that enough was enough. She was not putting up with it anymore, once again my mental health had got in to such a fragile state that she drove out to me to take me home. I had nothing, I left all my belongings behind and sat in the car in silence all the way home. I did not even wait to tell Bob, once again my Mum was my rock, I think she had wanted to do this for a long time, I think she thought it was going to be too good to be true. She was right of course, She had always made sure she was never relying on anyone especially a man with a gift of the gab.

A little while later when I felt up to it I returned to France to collect all my belongings and vowed never to put myself through something like that again. I found out that Bob was indeed seeing someone else from the Yacht club and had asked his wife to go with him to live in the barn, but she had refused. They saw him for what he was, I just saw a situation that I thought would allow me to start all over again with a new life, instead became a false hope and an eventual nightmare. Once again, I was too trusting.

So, months later I am trying to survive on odd jobs here and there, stuck in another pokey rabbit hatch called a flat with my son living with me. What do I do, life seems to have become a struggle, I am getting to an age where I should be settled, in a nice home with loving family and planning holidays. Instead I am picking up the local papers looking for jobs that no one else wants to do because the money is too crap. Then I saw it.

"Wanted Escorts, good rates of pay, start immediately call........"

Chapter 14 - Stepping up a Gear.

For the next few months Ricky would pick me up in his car and drive me around to various houses and flats to have variations of sex with different men. Each day I would dress up in my best smart but sexy attire, black stockings with high heels and make sure I was made up to the nines. Sometimes it was exciting, other times it was scary and some days I just went through the motions to get my money at the end of it. As much as I enjoyed the company of men, it was the money that I wanted. Men had continually been bad news in my life. Here was a way I kept independent while earning a good wage. I was not going to let any man ruin it for me. I had not turned into a man hater, I just did not trust my own judgement anymore when it came to relationships. This was a way of meeting men, sometimes having a good time but always getting well paid at the end of the job.

One thing that has never left me even from all those years ago, is the apprehension of going into a stranger's home to have sex with them. You would have to do this while being hyper sensitive about everything that is going on around you. One man could let you in but there be another four-upstairs ready to do unspeakable things to you. You just did not have a clue. Having a churning stomach while trying to be sexy and perform your job takes great strength of character. If you look nervous and worried the client will tell and he will not feel great about what is going on. Also, this person is allowing a total stranger into their home to have sex and he will not have a clue who is walking though that front door. I could have 3 big guys in the car ready to rob him! It's a very forced scenario and one you just must take a chance with. For some men, the whole stranger sex scenario is a huge turn on, but it was still always a good idea to keep your wits about you, after all it's a job and I there to perform as they wish.

After a short period, I began to drive myself to appointments, this meant losing a bit of security, but I tried to make sure I was aware of the situations I was walking into. The problem with doing the rounds was the gaps between appointments were a time I was not earning. I would be driving where Ricky directed me to go and then perform, get my money and off to the next one. I felt out of control, and I felt I should be earning more. Clearly, I was becoming addicted to the money. The one good thing about working the rounds was that the clients were known to Ricky and did not cause any problems. The only incident I had was when one client wanted to pay me by cheque. As usual I was a bit trusting and took the cheque. It was for over £100 and it bounced. I contacted Ricky and told him, his response was disappointing, "What do you want me to do about it? You took it."

So, I called the client up and told him to meet at The Half Way House Pub on the A127 with my cash or I will make his life hell. All the anger of past men ripping me off came to the surface and I was spitting fire. Thankfully he did turn up and sheepishly handed me the cash and that was the matter closed. Again, I was too trusting and even in this environment I let my guard down for one minute. It did not happen again.

After about 6 months I met some of the other girls who worked for Ricky and one of them told me about working in a brothel. She told me it was just down the road in Romford and there was a space opening. She told me how full on it was and the money was not that bad, but it was constant. It sounded like a very busy brothel indeed. Perhaps this was what I needed? I got hold of the phone number. I thought I would give it a go on my days off working for Ricky.

As the months passed by I got used to the regular money coming in. I did look to see if there was any other work that I could do to maybe ween me off the escorting, but nothing matched it. I could get a job cleaning, or cooking school dinners and though there is nothing wrong with that sort of work it just did not match anything near to what I was bringing home.

As time went on I decided I wanted to earn more. I had a one-track mind and it was to earn as much of my own money as I possibly could.

Each night I would go home to my one-bedroom house where my Son would be waiting for me. He would be worried for my safety every night. At first this lifestyle I had chosen had been our little secret. I did not want him to know at first, I thought I would get myself back on my feet and soon I would give up. He was supportive, and his main concern was that I was safe. It could not have been easy him knowing his mother was a prostitute, but he knew all the crap I had been put though and this seemed like the only way I was going to be able to pull myself back up and have the life I always wanted. There was no way I was going to allow another man into my life, I still felt burnt from what happened before. Now I was going to concentrate on me. Earn earn earn and earn some more. I know money doesn't buy happiness, but it enables you to be independent and this seemed at the time to be the only way for me.

Soon I contacted the brothel and spoken to a lady called Aussie Sandy. She had three brothels and told me to meet her at the one in Romford. The brothel was a flat above some shops in a high street, it had a reception room as you walked in and 2 bedrooms and a bathroom off to the side as well as a small kitchen. There was always a maid who was very important in the whole process. She kept the beds clean and made up as well as making sure there was food and drink available for all. She would also answer the security phone and allow the clients up the stairs into the flat. The client would sit in the reception area and both the girls would then parade themselves in front of him, introduce themselves in the most seductive way and then leave. The maid would then ask him to choose and then take the appropriate amount of money of them. She would then grab the appropriate girls account sheet and write in the time and amount paid so at the end of each day we knew exactly how much we had earnt.

Many of the clients wanted quickies, just blowjobs or quick fucks in their lunch breaks that sort of thing. So, each appointment would earn the house say £30, half of this would go to the house and the other half would be our own. They did however do a special deal where every tenth client you would get the full amount all to yourself. So, at the end of each night she would work out how much we earnt for ourselves and the house. Then out of our own money we would pay the security guy £20 each and then what was left after that was our own. You most definitely had to work hard to earn the money. The place was a conveyer belt of men, some days we would have thirty to forty guys a day which as you can imagine used to mount up, financially. It was both easy money as the clients would just come to us and incredibly hard work with the sheer volume of men that came through the door.

The other job the maid had was as a good time keeper, if you were to lose track of time during appointment she would knock on the door with 10 minutes to go so you knew you had to finish up soon.

I had one room and another girl would be in the other bedroom, so there would always be two girls working at one time. I thought this seemed quite good as it enabled you to talk to someone in between jobs, maybe have a laugh and help pass the time. It soon became apparent that we barely had time to freshen up in between men visiting us. We were either on the bed on our backs with our legs up around our ears or on all fours at one end or the other. We barely had time to have a cup of tea and this was literally every day I worked there.

It really was like working in a sex factory, the men poured in one by one or sometimes in small groups and we did what we had to do, took their money and everyone was happy. That was until we got raided by the Vice Squad. It always amazed me that the Police would have the cheek to raid us and close us down. Some nights they were our biggest clients and then another night they would come and close us down. It did not make sense to me, we were doing nobody any harm, the neighbours did not have much of a clue what was going on. We were quiet and never caused any problems at all. Then the knock on the door and the clients frog marched out the flat.

After a raid, we had to be out of the area for three months before we set up shop again and started the conveyer belt of men being pleasured again. This did not interrupt my earning potential too badly as Aussie Sandy had two other brothels not too far away, so we would just relocate there. I also worked a few days a week for Ricky. So, all in all I was earning very good money. I had become desensitised to what I was doing, each client was £20, £30 or £100 depending on time and what was required. My body had become my work tool of choice. I made sure I looked after it, always safe sex, no anal and nothing too rough. Some men would try to take the condom off when they were taking you doggy style, but I always checked by feeling his cock with my hand to make sure the slippery condom was still there. If it wasn't I would stop and make him put one back on. They hated it but there was no way I was going to put my life at risk just so it could feel a bit better for him. No Way.

During one of periods of time after the raids we were shipped off to Forest Gate to a horrible ground floor flat. The place had a tiny kitchen barely five feet square and mold in the bathroom and kitchen. It truly was a disgusting place, but surprisingly very busy. It had a maid and CCTV which we never had at Romford. We could see the guys waiting for us in the front room while were getting ready in the bedrooms.

One day I was sat on the bed just freshening up and then I heard the door buzzer go and I saw the maid open the door. I carried on getting ready and thought nothing off it. Suddenly I heard a scream and saw the maid being held up against the wall with a handgun to her head. She screamed for her life as I saw a second man taking the days takings from the drawer. When these thugs attacked a brothel, they would always just go for the maid. She was the one who knew everything, where the money was and if it was kept in a safe she would be the only one who knew the password. The other girl I worked with banged on the door and shouted, "For fucks sakes run." We did, I felt awful for the maid, but fear had over taken us, and we ran down the street as fast as we could. We got to a phone box and called Aussie Sandy. She did not seem surprised at all and just told us to leave it to her.

Soon I became aware of the 'flat' wars in the area. Other brothel owners would send guys like the two who attacked our flat to intimidate the girls and get them to close. Aussie Sandy was having none of this and would always be able to get new girls to work there when need be. She soon shipped me off to her other brothel in Seven Kings. This was on the main high street and you had to enter from behind the shops, through a dark alley and up some stairs. The flat was posh and much bigger and in a much better state. It had a Greek room with a jacuzzi, which was very popular with the clients and the girls were all made to wear evening wear like cocktail dresses and ball gowns.

Generally, the clientele was very nice, it was a relaxed atmosphere and everyone there would enjoy themselves. We would work until 1:30AM and it was a nice environment to make some good money. So, it caught us unawares one night after midnight when we were winding down. The maid had let two gentlemen in and Shirley the other girl I was working with watched on the cctv as the black and white guy came through the door. Soon one pulled a knife and the other pulled out a set of nun chucks and started swinging them about. We started to panic, Shirley started to scream and could not be calmed down at all. It was then I realised the predicament we were in as we could not get out the back as there was no door and the windows were all covered in security bars. We were trapped. Panic set in.

The black guy knew exactly who to go for and grabbed the maid, he knew to look for the sheets that kept account of how many clients had been through the flat that night and he saw it was a busy night. The problem was that Aussie Sandy arranged to have the money from each flat collected every few hours so there would not be large sums of money on site. The man did not believe her when she said it had been picked up. He got more and more irate. He threw the poor maid to the ground and then started making a bee line for us. First, he grabbed Shirley and took her hand bag off her, he tipped it upside down on the bed and all that fell out were a load of condoms and makeup. That is all she carried, you never had any I.D. or anything like that just good old condoms and makeup. He was getting angrier and turned to me. I had a small attaché case and he grabbed it. I started to get very angry and felt this was not right.

"You try and empty that and it will be the last thing you see." I said in my most stern voice possible.

"What?"

I held up my stilettos waving one in each hand as if to stab them. "I'll gouge your fucking eyes out." The black guy looked at me as if I was potty and still tried to grab the case.

"Anyway, I wouldn't if I was you, as you are both on candid camera mate." He looked around then started to get nervous. The white guy gestured to the other guy that they should leave and soon they bolted through the front door. As they left they locked the door.

We were trapped inside and had no means to get out. My biggest fear was that they might try and petrol bomb the flat and we would be burnt alive. I got on the phone and called Aussie Sandy, as usual she was all calm and said she will try and get there within the hour.

"Oh no you won't, "I shouted down the phone, "Get your arse here now." I was angry and frightened as we just did not have a clue what was going to happen. She agreed to come quickly and then said, "Romford got done as well tonight."

"Oh great, more flat wars is it?" I replied.

"Something like that."

It was during all this that I thought you do not own me. When you work for the brothels you feel like they have some sort of power over you. Without them and their flats you can't earn the money and without you they can't earn their money. I soon realised that I did not like working for someone else. Over the time, I worked with her I had lots of arguments with Aussie Sandy, she was horrible who treated the girls like crap. If we got hurt or scared and said we didn't like something that was going on, her response was that we could be replaced in an instant. So many girls wanted to earn the money we were, so there was no shortage of replacements if I left. That was exactly what I did, I left. I worked in a couple more places and while all this was going on I continued to work for Ricky. Even though we had our disagreements now and then, I realised that he was a good guy and when I needed to earn money he was always there.

Chapter 15 – Going It Alone.

Becoming an independent escort in those days was quite unheard of. You either worked for a brothel or an escort agency. They arranged all the adverts and dealing with bookings over the telephone. As an escort all you had to do was turn up, do what was wanted and leave. Each night you get your money handed to you and if you are reliable and the punters liked you, you got asked back. Most girls liked this, of course this came at a cost. A big chunk of your money would go back to the brothel or agency to cover the costs of this. Though this was understandable, I did feel that some of them took a bigger percentage than that was fair. I thought, I can do that, how hard can it be. I will get a flat of my own, place the adverts and deal with the calls and therefor keep all the money.

So, I rented a flat in Chadwell heath. It was a lovely flat that I decorated to an even higher standard. I was not going to work in another smelly mold filled shit hole, I wanted my place to reflect me, I wanted it to be classy and a place you feel you can relax and have a nice time. Soon I was seeing clients and I was as busy as ever, in fact I was getting too many clients wanting to come to my place. I thought it would be a good idea to arrange more girls to work with me. I heard about two girls looking for somewhere to work and said I only wanted 25% of their money. I was not going to take half their money as I thought a quarter was a fair amount for their rent and I paid for a security guy to be there also. Compared with all the other brothels it was bloody good deal.

They were only alone at the flat on Tuesday and Saturday as I took a job in a jewellers in Romford. I thought this was a good chance to do something different after my son Joe said they needed someone. They also paid me in jewellery which was very nice indeed. It was so nice to be thinking about other things, such as customers in the shop and how nice the display looked in the window.

Needless to say, the girls started lying about their earnings and I soon realised they were trying to take advantage of my good nature. I used to ring the flat up at various times of the day and if the phone was not answered I knew they were with a client. This was before the time of mobile phones, the phone was a house phone, so if they weren't working they would have answered. I used to compare the times I rang to their work sheets and I knew they were lying to me. The girls had to go.

It was a shame, but I was getting used to people trying to rip me off or take advantage of me, so I decided to cut all ties with working girls and brothels and worked from my flat alone. In my personal life things were good. I bought a house and my Mum could move in with me. My son, Joe had met someone new and was very happy, so things were looking up for me. When Mum moved in with me she did not know what I was doing but she was a sharp lady. She knew that when I got back from France I only had the clothes on my back and then barely a year or so later I have bought a house and I am going out dressed to the nines and coming home late every night.

I let slip one day about what I did and when I realised I felt a lump in my throat as awaited my mum's response.

"I knew you were doing something like that, "she said. From then on, she was brilliant about it all. She was very understanding and supportive and even would come up to the flat with me opening the door and making tea for the clients. They loved her, they would call her mum and have a great big laugh with her while they waited for me to be ready. She was so good with the clients, it was such a relief.

It was during this time that I had to tell my eldest son Jason what I did for a living. The reason being was that I was asked to be on a documentary on television about escorting. I really did not want him to find out what I did this way, so I arranged a time to sit down and discuss it with him. When I told him, he was not happy. He accepted it was what I did but said he did not have to like it. The main thing was that I told him and now it was all out in the open what I did. By and large everyone supported me, and it was such a relief that I could just be open about what I had started doing.

For 10 years the flat gave me a good living, I had no problems and lots nice regular clients that I built up over time. My own life was great with my relationship with my mum and rest of the family being good, so everything seemed run along nice and smoothly. It made a nice change. As another British winter came and went I decided now would be a good time to retire. It was 2006 and I was in my mid-fifties and there were hardly any escorts working at that sort of age. It was felt that at that sort of age you were passed it. I decided I would head off to warmer climes and lay on a beach and relax for a while. I decided I would head to Cyprus.

A friend of mine had a villa out there and said I could stay there to see how much I would like it there. I sold my house packed my bags and one incredibly hot August I flew out there. As much as I enjoyed the beaches, the food and the heat, I must admit I did get bored. After working full on as an escort, getting lots of attention from men to nothing I decided to place an advert in the local paper.

"Mature lady offering relaxing massage."

It cost me six Cypriot pounds and the response was quite good. Though I did not earn as much as in the UK, it kept me quite busy and it was nice to start meeting new people again. I also got a job working in the offices of a car hire firm locally, so It was not long before I became quite busy again. I enjoyed that very much. I got to meet many local men and we had a lot of fun.

One day I met a guy who told me that if I went home I would not have to place a small ad in the local newspaper again. When I asked him why he told me about a website called Adultwork. I had never heard of it, but he showed this website that was just made for escorts to advertise themselves no matter where they were. Long gone were the days of describing the girls over the phone. Now you could see profiles with loads of photographs, videos and all the likes and dislikes that she would perform for the client. You could book through the site and it made life so much easier for client and escort, it was brilliant. So, this guy set me up on there and I advertised my services on the website and men in the UK would book me for when they would come out on their holidays. It was great.

During this period, I learnt how to belly dance and was generally having a blast out there. Great wine, weather and lots of sex with lovely men who wanted to spend time with me. Then as usual with me things just imploded. Firstly, Cyprus introduced the Euro. When you are laying on the beach, relaxing with a nice cool drink and looking forward to meeting your next client, you do not really think about the country's economic policies, but ready or not the Euro came in and boy did it make a difference. Life became more expensive for everyone. Going to see an Escort dropped down most men's priorities and soon my client base dried up. It was like a huge switch had be turned off and soon the business ended.

This also coincided with other family problems. My son, Jason, had come out to Cyprus with his family and started working as a plasterer and was getting good work. Then slowly he fell into that trap that most ex pats seem to fall into and his whole life outside of work was based around booze. He had had drink problems in the past and we thought a change in his environment, nice beaches and weather would be a positive thing for him. Unfortunately for all this was not the case.

Soon he was drinking all the time, his wife was so worried. He drank and drove, turned up to my place at various times of day completely drunk and not in a good way. He is not a nice drunk to be around, but as his Mum I had to be there for him. He was losing work, so I gave him money to help him, but he used it for drink as I found out later. Soon his wife left him with the kids and came back to England. She just could not tolerate it anymore and so Jason was left in Cyprus with me. I really did not know what to do. My life became a nightmare. He seemed to be intoxicated all the time, in foul moods with his emotions about his wife leaving him. You really could not blame her. Soon my life went from blissful happy semiretired escort enjoying her life to a care worker for a drunk son. My life was a nightmare. With the Euro making life more and more expensive and no real reason to be there I decided to get Jason home to get him the help he needed. Being surrounded by 24-hour bars was not going to be of any help.

So, I had to pack everything up. The cost of having hauliers to ship my stuff back to the UK was expensive, so I sold off a lot of my stuff. I hardly had the money to fly home by this point. I got someone to transfer me some money over as I also had to get my dog back to the UK. This all proved to be somewhat expensive and so thankfully a good friend in England helped me out. Jason was very ill, he was yellow and incoherent a lot of the time and I knew if I did not get him home he would die.

The following days were a struggle. We made it onto the plane and got a cab to a good friend of mine called Terri. She said she would let us stay with her for a few days. We were so grateful. Jason just seemed to get worse and worse. He was withdrawing bad and I was really worried about him. Because I sold my house before moving out to Cyprus I had nowhere to go to on our return. I wish I had never sold up now, it was without doubt one of the biggest mistakes I made. Though thanks to Terri who worked in an estate agent, she found us nice little place to rent while we got ourselves back on our feet.

As usual my Mum came up with the deposit and soon we moved in with a few suitcases and nothing else what so ever. The place was in Stanford le Hope and though it was a nice little house, without all or stuff in storage we had no chairs to sit on or beds absolutely nothing. During all this Jason was flopping about all over the place. We had a terrible time trying to stop him from drinking or doing anything silly. We had a hard job trying to get him into a rehab. It seemed to take forever.

It took endless doctors' appointments before I could get the help Jason needed. Financially we were broke, I knew the social would not help me as I was classed as an alien due to being out of the UK for so long.

The problem I had also was I could not even do any escorting. I did not feel happy leaving Jason alone and also, I had nothing to work with in the house. No bed or chairs, I could expect someone to come and pay for sex on a rug in front of a dodgy gas fire, could I?

Over the next two years I got Jason in a rehab and I started working as an Escort in my new house. It was tough going back to it full time, especially after having months and months of hot beautiful sunshine and glorious beaches to end up returning to rainy England and the 'roll on roll off' brigade. It was a living, I should not complain but I tasted the good life and once again I found it all crashing down. So, I made do, I built up a client list again and used Adultwork for this which was incredibly helpful. It was quite unusual for a lady in her 50s to be an Escort. Men really wanted to pay for the hot firm bodies of eighteen-year old's and ladies in their early twenties, but a seismic change seemed to be happening. Men were seeking a woman who could chat as well perform in the sack, and sex and chatting are my two favourite past times. Soon men wanted MILF's, Moms I'd Like to Fuck as it is popularly known, women of a certain age, sexy, in good shape with a life experience that makes the whole experience less cold. It may be an act with some but just being yourself and knowing how much to be open with a client to make it feel more personal is a great asset to have. Soon I was as busy as I wanted to be, I was in the driving seat, I worked when I wanted and stopped when I wanted. It was working out quite well.

Even when my Landlord wanted to sell my house, it was a pain but not a setback. I found a place in Wickford, just a few more miles into Essex and continued with my work as if nothing had happened. It was really a good time for me. After some time, all my family had moved to the other side of the Thames into Kent and asked me if I would join them and be nearer. I liked that idea, having to drive through the tunnel and over the bridge from Essex to Kent was a pain for all so it seemed like a good thing to do. I was confident I would continue to work, even moving to another county and losing most of my regular clients.

I found a nice house, nice and discreet and ideal for me and I have lived here ever since. Thankfully Jason made a good recovery despite a few relapses now and then. It was so hard watching him destroy himself, especially when you know what a lovely guy he is and thankfully still is. So being closer seemed to be a good move for us all.

Chapter 16 - Surprises.

After working so long working as an Escort it is no wonder I have met my fair share of, shall we say, weirdos? The thing is a lot of the time you think you know what is going to happen. A blowjob, shag from behind, me on top, all the usual positions everyone has come to love. However, every now and then there is always someone who catches me unawares.

I go into most situations with my radar working, looking and searching for anything that shouldn't be there or something that feels different. Like it or not I am putting my life on the line with every meeting I arrange. I had or have no intention of being another sex worker statistic that gets swept under the carpet when it happens.

So, an Indian man had been calling me loads to meet up. He kept talking to me but never had the guts to actually commit to an appointment. To be honest I thought he was just having a wank on the end of the phone each time he called m. I decided that next time I was going to hang up on him, but he finally said a time and date to meet. He wanted to book a £40 session. So not long but a booking is a booking.

He finally turned up and went into the room, and I spoke to my security man for a second and then followed him in. As I entered he was naked except for a pair of marigold gloves. He lay there aroused, scrunching his fingers back and forth to get the fingers into the gloves properly. I looked at him and asked him, "What are the gloves for?"

He looked at me and as calm as day said, "They are for touching your body, I mean after all you are a whore, so you are dirty."

Well I lost it, I went mad. I stared him in the eye and said, "I know what I am, but I am not dirty you bastard." I got the security guard and told him to get rid of him. He tried to run out with his trousers around his ankles and his marigolds still on his hands, he looked a right sight as I threw his money back at him and watched him try to pick it up with the gloves on. That really go my goat.

He never called back.

Not long after I got a call from a man called Richard, or so he said his name was Richard and he asked me to do something strange for him. He booked a time and date and said between now and then would I keep all the used condoms used by my clients and keep them in the fridge until he came to his booking. He said when he got here he would tell me what to do next. So, clients would come and go, and I would offer to take their condoms for them by placing them in a plastic box and storing them in the fridge. I did not feel at ease with this, but once again a booking is a booking and I did agree with the request. So now my plastic box is full of sperm filled condoms in my fridge next to the salad spinner awaiting to find out what happens next.

So, he turns up, very nicely dressed and well spoken. He came in and said, "May I have the box of condoms please?"

So, I went to the fridge, got the box out as walked it over to him. He laid all the condoms out on a tray pulled out a pair of scissors and a glass. He then removed his jacket, trousers, underpants and shoes and sat in the chair. My heart was pounding now as I still had no real idea what he was going to do. I did actually charge quite a bit extra to do this but wished I hadn't now. He grabbed three condoms and started to rub them on my boobs. It was cold and slippery and to be honest I was totally gagging. How I did not throw up I never know. Especially as he got another condom and snipped the end off and started to massage the sperm into his own cock and balls. I could see he was really getting off on it and he rubbed himself with all the cold sperm.

He got hold of the glass and handed it to me. "Can you wee in the glass please?"

"What?"

"Wee, can you wee in the glass please?"

"In front of you?"

"Yes please," he said. I can tell you now it is so difficult to wee into a glass when someone is staring at you. I put the glass between my legs and tried to relax. I thought of streams, fountains and God knows what else to try and get anything out. Soon a trickle of wee flowed into the glass and soon I was handing it back to him. I was just hoping he was not expecting me to do anything with it. He took the glass and sat down on the floor, his privates all covered in sperm, placed the glass to his mouth and drank it. He just knocked it back like a spirit from the pub. I heaved, I tried to hide my disgust from my face and I am not sure if I did a good job or not, but it was all I could do from actually vomiting in front of him. It was probably best I didn't just in case he wanted to eat that up as well. I mean, you just don't know do you?

During all this time I have not even touched him. He was so aroused, I did not need to touch him. He positioned himself in such a way that he looked at me while he masturbated. His hand got faster and faster until he came, and the sperm shot straight into his mouth. I kid you not, like a sick erotic circus act he knew exactly what position he need to be in to ejaculate into his mouth. During the whole process he wanted me to call him names and humiliate him. So in between me retching I would call him a "Sick Fuck, "You Dirty Bastard." Which I was actually thinking as it goes so it was a genuine humiliation. The thing was at the flat he visited I was the only who would consider his request. As usual the extra money made me go that extra mile and sometimes I wish I knew when to say no. The thing was there was no sex on my part, I just had sperm on my boobs and had to call him names. But each time he came back I really had to psych myself up to go through with it with him. He would give me notice to collect the condoms and then I would store them in my fridge. It was easy enough getting all the condoms, once a man has shot his load he generally wants to get dressed and go. He isn't with me looking to discuss the state of the world, he wants sex and go. So, whipping the slipping condoms of his deflating condom was both appreciated by them and easy for me. Off he goes, and another sperm filled condom goes into my special Tupper ware box sitting on the top shelf of the fridge. Right next to the Dairy Lea Triangles and milk. Sometimes they would sit there for a week or more. I felt he was taking his life into his own hands, he did not have a clue whose sperm it was or if there was anything wrong with them. He just did not care. I could never look my fridge in the same way again.

As with all business's dealing with people, you have to deal with all sorts. You have the silent ones, they turn up do the business and go. Some have a look of shame or embarrassment on their face as they leave. It is as if there only way to fulfil a need was to see a prostitute and were embarrassed to do so.

Others are full of it on the phone, they tell how good it's going to be, what they are going to do and then never show up. It is really annoying for me, as they do not tell you they aren't coming they just do not bother. All mouth and no trousers, drives me nuts.

There are those who have had bad experiences with Escorts, they have been mugged or ripped off and the men are very wary of what will happen. Or you will get the idiots who want to pull the condom off while you are bent over so they can have sex with you bareback. Why? I am sure it feels better, but they must realise that it can be fun and safe. Why put your life or someone else's life at risk like that?

Chapter 17 – Men

I look back over my life and to coin a phrase, it is a game of two halves. The first half was my life being involved with users, con men, men you just could never trust in a month of Sundays. I fell for the bad boys, perhaps I thought I could change them, or I would enjoy their way of life. They had the gift of the gab, they said lovely things to me and swept me off my feet only for everything go down the tubes as it was all lies.

Every time I would give up control of my finances I would end up with nothing. He would be drunk, gambling or just doing something illegal that I would end up spending time inside. Don't get me wrong I was no angel, but I do think my willingness to trust and give everyone the benefit of the doubt cost me so much.

When I look back to France, freezing, almost starving because I was left there while my so-called boyfriend was at home in the warm having a lovely meal with his wife. I cannot even believe I fell for it. It's no wonder I finally learnt my lesson and feel I will never be able to trust a man for a relationship again. Yes, I was stupid, but each time I believed I was going to finally have a better life.

The second half of my life started out as a necessity. I needed to earn money. I could have and did have various jobs, but I could never ever earn that amount of money so quickly. I became greedy, I wanted more and more. Men came to me for sex, they gave me money for my time and we had a nice time and off they went, then the next and the next. The thing is a lot of these men are actually very nice. Some demand things as they are paying for my time and feel I should do anything they want but they are few and far between. Most want the experience to fun, friendly and sexy and that suits me down to the ground.

So, my attitude towards men is simple now, I will always be on my guard, I will not trust you, but you will not know that I don't trust you unless you try to do something stupid. If I do not want to do what you want I will say no, I am now in control and it feels good.

I felt like I first took full control of my life when I started Escorting. In the early days in the brothels or even visiting clients in their homes you felt you had to do everything they wanted. If you didn't then you may lose your job. This was ridiculous of course, there was always work for escorts of any age. Through life it is always ingrained into you to work, to do a good job, keep the boss happy and do whatever you are told to make the money. I soon realised when it's your body that makes the money, you must be safe, make sure you only do what you want to do or indeed what you enjoy doing. No one owns me, they have my time and we will see what happens. I want it to be a special time for those who I meet, but only on my own agreed terms.

That's another thing that the internet can be good for, setting out your stall to exactly what you offer so there is no excuse when the client turns up and he asks for something you do not wish to do. I am sure many clients just flick through the photographs but then it down to them if they do not get what they want.

Advertising on the internet, especially on Adultwork, has opened a whole new world in the sex industry. You can find a man or woman that matches your taste. This has allowed men who prefer larger ladies, older ladies or ladies of a certain ethnicity to find whatever they like. No more meeting someone who they have not got a clue what they look like. Of course, I am sure there are fake profiles, but by and large it has made finding the right Escort a lot easier.

This of course has given rise to the GILF. A Granny I'd like to Fuck. You can be a Granny these days from forty years old which is still a MILF in my book. A Granny I feel should be in her fifties or older. Anyone who saw me on TV in My Granny the Escort, will know there are ladies in their eighties doing this sort of work, and why not?

I say good luck to them, I hope I am able to do it when I am their age. I guess the big question is, will I still be doing it? And to be honest I have not got a clue. Right now, I can pick and choose my clients, work when I want, go away when I want and spend time with my family when I want. So right now, I seem to have found a good balance of work and life.

Do I still have any more ambitions in my life? Yes, I do, I do have a burning ambition, an itch if you will, that I really need to scratch. I want to do some more TV work. Why not? After all I am only sixty-seven years old, that's still a spring chicken these days, isn't it?

Chapter 18 – A Star is Born.

In 2003, I was working in my flat in Essex, humping away and just getting on with things as usual. It was just another normal day, then the phone rang. Nothing unusual about that, I thought it was another client wanting to book himself a lovely time with me, but I was wrong. It was Channel 4 asking me if I would like to be involved in the making of a documentary called "Personal Services." Needless to say, I was a bit sceptical and did think it could have been a wind-up call. So, they gave me a number to call and a meeting was arranged. It then turned out to be a genuine offer to be in a television documentary about ladies who work in the sex industry. There were to be others, Madam Becky with Kitten her sub, and a lady from Reading and another lady called Charlie who owned a few flats that were used as brothels.

When they began filming I was decorating my flat, this did not seem to bother them as long as I was working at the same time. At first, I thought, "Oh no what have I agreed to?" I knew everyone would know what I did now, and did I want that? Then I thought more about it and decided I did not want to live a lie anymore. I wanted the world to see that we were normal people providing a good service and what we did was a good thing and not some seedy horrible process that many imagined it to be.

Soon the camera man and sound guy seemed to blend into the background and acted very professionally. They were not intrusive at all. All they asked was that they could film a client paying me before we went off to the bedroom, he agreed and they said they would blur his face out and everything worked out great. I had some positive responses from this, but I was more pleased that they did not try and edit my message out about the good that we do.

Next, I got a call from TLC television channel to see if I would be ok to be interviewed for their program. They did not seem too bothered that I had just finished one documentary and sent a crew around to my house. I was to be interviewed by Jodie Marsh, at first, I did not know what to expect. I only knew of her what I saw in the newspapers, so I kept an open mind.

She turned up with her crew and it was bloody awful. She could not remember her lines, the filming had to be continually stopped so they could tell her what she had to say. In the end she had to hold the script in her hand so she could not forget what she was asking. It became quite embarrassing after a while.

Just to add insult to injury she was quite rude and talked about my work in a rather derogatory way. When her narration was placed over the documentary she called escorts "the lowest of the low." Not very nice, makes you wonder why she bothered making the documentary at all. When she posed in the window in Amsterdam, she was very rude to the men who eyed her up through the glass. She called them perverts and rapists. It was a shockingly bad documentary and just used as a platform for her TV career at all our expense.

Soon the phone went again, and I was asked to go on 'Trisha'. Again, I felt very positive as it was another chance to get my message across and show it is a genuine service that is needed. I was on stage with Madam Becky. Before we went on stage, Trisha popped her head around the door and said, "I am Trisha, I will be asking the questions." Then pulled the door shut. It was not very friendly, and I had a bad feeling about this.

We both sat on the stage and it was a very judgemental and hostile crowd. One woman said I should not being doing such a thing as a granny who takes money for sex. I responded and said, "Well what do you do?"

"I am a housewife and look after my kids."

"So that's your job?"

"Yes, yes, it is."

"So, who gives you housekeeping to get the shopping and things for the kids?"

"Well, my husband."

"Do you have sex with him?"

She looked stunned, I answered for her. "Of course, you do, you got kids. So, you are no better than me. We both give sex and we both get money."

The crowd cheered, and I have to be honest I was rather pleased with myself. It shut her up but still the hostilities continued all through the interview even with questions from Trisha.

I felt like my TV appearances would be over now, to be honest I didn't care. Every time escorting was brought up anywhere there would always be a negative response or rude comments. Especially about my age and still doing it. I needed something to regain my trust in humanity, something special. It came, and it was going to be Eamonn & Ruth.

The researchers for This Morning, contacted me and asked if I would be interviewed on their show. I asked by whom and they said Philip Schofield and Holly Willoughby and I refused. I had seen them in similar interviews being really rude and negative about the person they were talking to. I told this to the researcher and she said, "Would you like to come back the week after? It's Eamonn and Ruth."

I immediately said yes. I knew if there was a chance to getting a fair hearing it would be with these two. I was also a big fan of them both, so I hoped it would be a good experience.

I met the researchers and they asked me a few questions to prepare, then sound check. It was all very nerve wrecking and knees were trembling

Eamonn and Ruth checked on me in the green room where I sat with Caroline Quentin and they were so supportive. Caroline said I was providing a service for older people, disabled and those who just did not want to be involved in a relationship. I did feel a bit more at ease I must say. So nice to have positive vibes all around me.

After Caroline I was ushered on to the stage and before I knew it I was live on TV with Eamonn and Ruth. It took me a while to get going as my nerves were getting the better of me but before you knew it we were having a good old chin wag and the whole experience was so uplifting. They really allowed me to get my message across and I will always be grateful for that.

A bit more time past and once again I got a call from Channel 4 to make a documentary called "My Granny the Escort."

Charlie Russell met me and told me that it would be focused on 3 mature escorts, one who was 57, another who was 80 and myself. We negotiated a price and I agreed to be filmed. No script he said, just chat. Now that is easy for me, anyone who knows me will know that I can chat the hind legs off a donkey.

This turned out to be another great experience. The film crew were brilliant, and Charlie was very easy to work with. I hardly noticed they were there. We filmed so much stuff it was a shame they had to cut so much due to time restraints.

Soon it was shown on Channel 4 and the response was incredible. Most seemed to focus on the 80-year-old lady and then there a lot of focus on myself. Some negative as you would expect but a lot more positive. It was soon shown all around the world and people contacted me with words of support, it was amazing. I really got the bug for this TV work and would love to do more.

Chapter 19 – Switch on Bev TV

My digital career is going to explode, hopefully. I have decided to drag my bum into the 21st century and start my own YouTube channel. It is called Bev's Place. It is not just a self-promotional thing for my escorting but a genuine channel for people of a similar age who feel that sex is over for them.

Sex is different now, more relaxed, more tantric, more fun. More chatting more fun and just general fun and enjoying themselves. I think as we get older people forget this. You have your own pace, your new likes and dislikes. Through my blog of the same name I want to keep couples and singles of a certain age, let's face it I mean over sixty, having great sex. There is no reason why you cannot. It just takes a little bit more time, imagination and relaxation. The days of jumping off wardrobes and swinging from the light fittings are well and truly over but pleasure seeking and giving are not.

I have a lot of experience of dealing with older men in these situations and as a mature lady I can share my techniques of how to pleasure your man. On the flip side I know what I like so I can show all the men out there how to keep pleasing their lady even when things do not work like they once did.

Time will always beat us in the end, so it is paramount that we enjoy every minute we are given and spending it having great sex is definitely a good thing to do.

So, a channel specifically aimed at sex lives of the over 60s is quite unique and I hope will become very popular. So, I am keeping everything crossed, except my legs of course, that would be silly.

Chapter 20 – My Biggest Support, My Rock, My Mum.

All through my life the greatest influence, support and best friend was my mother. There is not a day that goes by where I do not think of her. When I was younger and going through my lashing out teenage years she was always there. She made sure I knew I was loved and cared for. Even as I got older and ended up in poor relationships she was there for me, offering me a bed, money or a great big cuddle. She loved her grandkids and even though she could be stern and scary for a little boy she stood in for me a few times and took care of them for me.

She seemed to hoover up all my mistakes and help me get a fresh clean slate to reboot my life again. Even when I started escorting and I was too terrified to tell her, deep down she knew. She was living with me in those early days and saw my go out at funny times all dressed up to the nines and coming home late at night with a purse full of cash. When I finally plucked up the courage to tell her response was priceless. She knew. She always knew.

Soon she showed her support to me by making clients big mugs of tea as they waited for me to get ready for their appointment, she would laugh and joke with them and really make them feel at home. I think that was another magical thing about my mum, she always knew the right thing to say regardless of the situation.

She shocked me once by saying, if she had her time all over again she would have become an escort as well. I was not sure if she meant that or not or was just showing her support for what I ended up doing for a living. Without her it would have been a lot harder to do for this length of time. Soon, glamour magazines with older ladies was becoming more and more popular and I was offered a few shoots. She would make or put together clothes to ensure the shoot was more sexy, classy or just different. She was so artistic and loved designing and making clothes.

Even when we were apart, and I was in that hell hole situation in France it was my mum that sent the money and got me back home. How could I lean on her so much? The thing is, she was my mum and she always said she would do anything for me, and she did. She was an inspiration to me. When Jason became an alcoholic all I could think was what can I do to make this right. It was tough, I thought I would lose him and fought with doctors and other professionals to get him assessed and in the right place. I know if it was me, my mum would have done the same for me.

In her later life, she had a few relationships with some men, some I liked others I didn't, but we were always there for each other. She moved in with me and finally I got the chance to look after her. She wanted for nothing She would come to the flat I worked at, or ring me to make sure I was safe or wait up until I got home to make sure I had another successful and safe day.

One of the most difficult times with my mum was when a family secret came out in the open. Aunty Cheryl and I had always got on, like most we had ups and downs and sometimes things were said that seemed to be a little bit strange. We were sometimes referred to as, "The Girls."

Nothing sinister in that, I just assumed we were treated the same as were of a similar age.

Then one day, Cheryl's daughter decided to explore the family tree. This then prompted my mum to call me and tell me she needed to speak to me about something. I was obviously intrigued as I could detect concern in her voice. This was unusual as she was always strong, and nothing seemed to phase her, but this time it was different.

"There is no other way I can say this, Cheryl is your sister." It was like a slap on the face. I never expected her to say that, all my life she had been Aunty Cheryl. Now I find out we are half-sisters. It really was a huge shock. My mum had had a relationship with an American serviceman and Cheryl came along as a result. In those days you could not be an unmarried mother, if it happened it was common place for the pregnant lady to give the child to another family member to be brought up by. In this case it was my Nan and Grandad.

Though she was brought up well and had a good life, they were very strict with her and did not give her freedom and happiness that my mother bestowed upon me. Cheryl resented me for this and could not forgive my mum for giving her up. The problem was when my mum got married and gave birth to me, my Grandparents would not give her up and kept her.

As a result of this, Cheryl felt let down by my mum, she felt as though she had been dumped and forgotten about. It must be an awful feeling to not only be given up but to not know who your father is. Not knowing part of your roots, where you have come from must be a horrid feeling.

So now I had a sister, her daughter Nichola who started the family tree, went from being a cousin to a niece, as did Tracey in one foul swoop, it was all very awkward. Despite all this coming to light, Cheryl and I get on really well and it has definitely not come between us.

When we lost our mum, it was like having my insides ripped out. She was very much part of me, a rock not just for me but the whole family. She loved them all and they loved her too, it was a very difficult time. The only comfort I had was that she lived the life she wanted. She always wanted to be a nurse and she was, she had her own business at the kennels and enjoyed her life to the full when she could. Even with all the nonsense that happened with my Dad, she was still happy.

She always remained as independent as possible right up till the end. She always had her own income and never relied on any man for anything. I wished I learnt that from her a lot earlier in life. My life might have gone a bit smoother. Who knows? I think she was very much the old school parent. She would let me get on with my life, make my own decisions and be there for me when it all went wrong. Which thankfully she was. She told me she was proud of me and loved me and I know I can say without doubt that I had the best mum in the world ever.

Chapter 21 - Reflections.

So, for once I sit here in my front room looking forward, it is a nice change from looking back and wondering what the hell I was doing? I lean back in my comfy sofa with a nice cup of tea and a biscuit and wonder to myself, what is going to happen next?

I have just come back from a safari in Kenya, all paid for by a client. It really was a trip of a lifetime. The man who took me seemed very nice, we had been chatting a while before he booked it. I did wonder at first if all men were like this how different my life would have been. As the trip progressed he started to try and get a bit more controlling, he started to sound more and more aggressive if things were not to his liking. I would apologise and say sorry and thankfully the bulk of the holiday was over when his controlling side started to show itself. It was a side I did not like.

When we got back to the airport, we got driven to Ebbs Fleet Railway Station and we said our goodbyes and then the texts and phone calls started to come in. He wanted a relationship. Oh crap. Thirty years ago, I may well have said yes. I did see good in him, he could be a gentleman and show a lady a very nice time. However, over time his dark aggressive side became more and more apparent and for once in my life I listened to the little voice in my head and said, "No." It took me nearly seventy years but there was no way I was going to have a relationship with a guy who shouts, stamps his feet and gets angry when things do not go his way.

In all honesty I feel I am way too selfish to have a Man in my life. I remember when I was working in the flats in Romford I met a guy called Barry, he was a client and for some reason I took a sort of a shine to him. We started to date and soon I was moving in with him. I still worked at the flats and it was not long before we realised that we both wanted different things in life. I was enjoying my work as an Escort, but naturally he wanted me to give it up. It is obvious when you look at it, why would any man want to be in a relationship with a woman who has sex with strangers for a living? It is not an unreasonable request if feelings start creeping into the relationship and it was then I realised I could never give it up. I love the money, the sex and buzz from meeting new clients and the fun of it all. Now I am in complete control of my life. In my own way my life is almost perfect. I have a wonderful family, some amazing friends all who have accepted me for who I am. Even Barry and I are still friends despite things not working out between us.

My family never judged me, we had ups and downs, but all families do. We have always been there for each other and I am very proud of my boys. We have all been dealt bad hands but managed to get through all the adversity. I am sure they wished their mum could have done something else with her life, to be honest so do I, but it was a way out. My life was spiraling out of control and the only way I could get control back was to support myself financially and be independent. Yes, I became addicted to the quick money, and when I learnt the ropes to become an independent escort it all worked out for me. I was not hurting anyone, I have always been respectful, I gained control for my life and that has been so important for me.

So, there I was on safari, experiencing the amazing scenery, wild life and culture. It would have been easy to let my guard down but for once I did not. I put myself first, and here I am happy with no stress and still enjoying life.

So, I have a booking with a sweet old regular today, the kettle is on the biscuits are laid out on a plate. I am all ready to spend a lovely time with him.

Yes, life is good.

-

Links to my work and blog.

My Blog.
https://beverlymerrindempsey.wordpress.com/2017/07/29/first-blog-post/

Escorting.
http://www.adultwork.com/ViewProfile.asp?UserID=529497

Printed in Great Britain
by Amazon